T5-DHC-668

WHERE
TO PUT
YOUR
MONEY
1987

Treasury notes — irs the best

Other books by Peter Passell

PERSONALIZED MONEY STRATEGIES:
15 No-nonsense Investment Plans to Achieve Your Goals

HOW TO READ THE FINANCIAL PAGES

WHERE TO PUT YOUR MONEY 1987

Peter Passell

WARNER BOOKS

A Warner Communications Company

Copyright © 1984, 1985, 1986, 1987 by Peter Passell and Cloverdale Press
All rights reserved.

Warner Books, Inc., 666 Fifth Avenue, New York, NY 10103

W A Warner Communications Company

Printed in the United States of America
First Printing: February 1987
10 9 8 7 6 5 4 3 2 1

Library of Congress Cataloging-in-Publication Data

Passell, Peter.
  Where to put your money, 1987.

  1. Finance, Personal—United States. 2. Investments—
United States. 3. Bank accounts—United States.
I. Title.
HG179.P27 1987   332.6'78   86-28917
ISBN 0-446-38497-6 (U.S.A.) (pbk.)
      0-446-38498-4 (Canada) (pbk.)

ATTENTION: SCHOOLS AND CORPORATIONS

Warner books are available at quantity discounts with bulk purchase for educational,
business, or sales promotional use. For information, please write to: Special Sales
Department, Warner Books, 666 Fifth Avenue, New York, NY 10103.

ARE THERE WARNER BOOKS YOU WANT
BUT CANNOT FIND IN YOUR LOCAL STORES?

You can get any Warner Books title in print. Simply send title and retail price, plus 50¢ per
order and 50¢ per copy to cover mailing and handling costs for each book desired. New
York State and California residents, add applicable sales tax. Enclose check or money
order—no cash, please—to: Warner Books, PO Box 690, New York, NY 10019. Or send for
our complete catalog of Warner Books.

CONTENTS

	Easy Access/Low Penalty	Risk of Loss	Return on Investment	Tax Shelter	Minimum Investment $	Good for Retirement Account?	Page Reference
Bank NOW Accounts	best	none	low	none	500	no	9
Bank Money Market Accounts	best	none	med	none	1,000	yes	10
Money Market Funds	best	low	med	none	1,000	yes	10
Passbook Savings	good	none	low	none	none	no	7
U.S. Savings Bonds	fair	none	med	some	25	no	19
U.S. Treasury Bills	good	none	med	some	10,000	yes	20
U.S. Treasury Notes	good	low	med	some	1,000	yes	20
Bank Savings Certificates (CDs)	good	none	med	none	500	yes	22
Intermediate-Term Bond Funds	best	low	med	none	1,000	yes	25
U.S. Treasury Bonds	good	med	high	some	1,000	yes	28
Other Government Bonds	fair	med	high	some	1,000	yes	30
Corporate Bonds	fair	med	high	none	1,000	yes	31
Long-Term Bond Funds	good	med	high	none	1,000	yes	32
Long-Term Unit Trusts	good	med	high	none	1,000	yes	32
Zero-Coupon Securities	fair	med	high	none	250	yes	33
GNMA Pass-Through Certificates	good	med	high	none	25,000	yes	36
GNMA Funds	good	med	high	none	1,000	yes	36
Tax-Exempt Bonds	fair	med	high	yes	1,000	no	41
Tax-Exempt Bond Funds	good	med	high	yes	1,000	no	47
Tax-Exempt Unit Trusts	good	med	high	yes	1,000	no	47
Deferred Annuities	fair	low	high	some	5,000	no	50
Universal Life Insurance	poor	low	high	some	1,000	no	52
Common Stock Mutual Funds	good	med-high	med-high	some	1,000	yes	61

1

INTRODUCTION

NOT LONG AGO, the choice was simple: Earn 5.25 percent from the corner savings and loan, or give the money to Uncle Ed the stockbroker, who put it in telephone company stock—or perhaps in a nice, safe tax-free municipal bond. But years of deflation, deregulation, and now tax reform have made investing as confusing as a first trip on the Los Angeles freeways. Banks, mutual funds, money market funds, bond specialists, stockbrokers, and the new "financial supermarkets" offer small savers a bewildering, ever-growing choice of ways to invest. Sweeping tax reform has created new opportunities . . . and new risks. Even Uncle Ed's favorite, doughty old Ma Bell, has been made over as a bunch of go-go stocks sporting names like NYNEX and Pacific Telesis.

How to choose? With the world of personal finance changing so rapidly, even the best standard investment guides are about as much use in deciding between a deferred annuity and a zero-coupon municipal bond as the 1907 edition of the Sears catalog. If you're the type who winters in Palm Springs or replaces the family Mercedes when the oil needs to be changed, no doubt you can also afford advice from an independent professional. But for most of us, who are rightly leery of suggestions from brokers and bankers with specific products to sell, the options are limited.

Enter *Where to Put Your Money*. This guide won't tell you whether hi-tech stocks are going up, whether platinum futures are going down, or whether Sheik Yamani will soon be heading for Switzerland. But for conservative investors with five, fifteen, or fifty thousand dollars, it offers simple, up-to-date advice on getting your money's worth. First, a few pointers on what can make an investment better or worse for you. Then, the specifics of what to buy and how to buy it. Very little jargon, no theory, midterm exam optional.

Really in a rush? The table in this introduction summarizes the savings choices described later on, rating each by the criteria that matter most. Then, at the end of each of the following chapters are a few handy tips on how to make your money work harder for you.

Getting it back can be as important as lending it out. . . .

In a hurry to pay that overdue bill for little Jennifer's orthodonture? You might sell the antique diamond brooch Aunt Alice left you in her will, accepting a lot less than the jewels are really worth. But think how much nicer it would be to have immediate access, without penalty, to the cash you need.

Sounds obvious. But, surprisingly, many investors, lured by promises of high returns on gemstones or real estate or other "illiquid" investments, allow themselves to be caught short in emergencies. Even people with minimal family responsibilities should keep their first $5,000 of savings in an easily accessible form and perhaps another $5,000 in automatic borrowing rights through a bank or credit cards.

"Churning" is a four-letter word. . . .

It does nice things for cream. But it can be death to your net worth. In most cases where you sell one kind of security in order to replace it with another, you lose money. Sometimes the cost of the transaction is very small—for example, just a few days' interest lost waiting for the checks to clear when you move cash from one money market fund or bank account to another. Usually it is modest—2 or 3 percent of the principal in fees. But use the same nest egg to buy and sell securities half a dozen times a year and the costs can easily exceed your investment earnings.

There is no lesson here worth carving in granite. Some people actually make money (or at least toasters and portable vacuum cleaners) by churning, taking advantage of premium rates or free gifts offered by banks to those who open new accounts. More important, if you find you've made a bad investment or are suddenly offered a better one, it often makes sense to pay the necessary price to change investment gears. Be careful, though, to take into account the cost of getting in and getting out before you buy. And be wary of brokers and salesmen who are perpetually coaxing you into this hot stock or that cool deal. Their gain could easily be your loss.

There are risks and there are risks. . . .

Say you go to a broker and buy an Exxon Corporation bond paying 10

2

percent interest for the next twenty years. There's some risk the company will fail to make the semiannual interest payments, or fail to return the money you invested when the bond is due for redemption in the year 2007. That's called "risk of default," and in Exxon's case it is probably very small, (a) because Exxon is a well-managed company selling a product that isn't likely to go out of style and (b) because the company's obligation to pay is backed by assets—refineries, ships, oil reserves—that exceed its debts. But there is another, far more serious risk to owning bonds and most other securities. Business school types call it "market risk."

The bond, you remember, is an agreement by Exxon to pay $100 in interest every year, then return the $1,000 principal twenty years from now. Suppose, though, money becomes "tight" in the economy next year and the interest rates offered to savers on new investments skyrocket to 20 percent. Suppose, in other words, that blue chip corporate borrowers like Exxon must promise to pay $200 interest annually on each $1,000 bond to induce investors to lend them more money. Exxon is still obliged to pay only $100 annually to owners of the old 10 percent bonds. So the old bonds are suddenly worth far less. Who, after all, would lend $1,000 to earn $100 a year when it is possible to lend the same $1,000 to the same corporation and earn $200 a year?

Risk linked to changes in market interest rates is a two-way street. Say interest rates in the economy go down rather than up, falling from 10 percent to 5 percent. Now your 10 percent bond will be worth a lot more than the $1,000 originally invested, because newly issued bonds will pay less interest.

But it's hardly surprising that most of us prefer less market risk to more. And, happily, there are ways to cut such risk. One is to buy securities that promise to return the full principal invested whenever you ask. U. S. government savings bonds provide this advantage; so do most certificates of deposit and money market accounts offered by banks, savings and loan associations, and credit unions. Typically, though, withdrawal of money from these investments carries some financial penalty; read more about them in the following chapters—*and always read the fine print before you sign on the dotted line*.

A second way to cut market risk is to buy securities that "mature" quickly. An Exxon bond paying 10 percent interest, due to be paid off next year, would fall very little in value even if interest rates rose to 20 percent. That's because Exxon is obliged to return the full $1,000 principal very quickly, allowing you to reinvest the money at a higher yield in short order.

A third way—really a close relative to the second—is to buy securities

3

in which the interest paid goes up and down with market rates. Money market funds constantly adjust the interest rate they pay to reflect competitive market rates, allowing them to guarantee a full return of your principal at any time.

Yet a fourth way is to make an investment backed by a specific guarantee against the loss of principal. Certificates of deposit (CDs) from banks allow you to withdraw all your money at any time with the payment of an interest penalty. So do U. S. savings bonds and a few, more complicated investments such as the "put" bonds and deferred annuities described in later chapters.

There's more to shelter than a roof over your head. . . .

Once it was the exclusive domain of fast-talking Texas wildcatters, California shopping center hustlers, and aging heiresses with triplexes on Fifth Avenue. Then it became a national obsession, rivaling Don Johnson's wardrobe and Vanna White's cleavage as subjects for backyard barbecue chatter. Then, suddenly, it evaporated, as the tax reform fever made the subject seem almost unpatriotic.

But hang on. The Internal Revenue Service certainly hasn't been abolished. And some forms of shelter from taxation live on. Indeed, the surviving strategies for conservative middle-income investors look healthier than ever. They work on one of two simple principles.

Tax deferral: Say you invest $1,000 in U.S. savings bonds that yield a minimum 7.5 percent annually, if held for long periods. Cash them in ten years later, pay the maximum 28 percent tax rate on the earnings, and you'll end up with $1,783.

Now try the experiment again. Invest the same $1,000 in a bank savings certificate that pays an equivalent rate of interest. Reinvest the earnings each year at the same average return, and you would accumulate a total of $1,704.

Why the $79 difference? The taxes on the interest earned on the savings bond are deferred until you cash them in, allowing the money to compound at the maximum rate. With the bank deposit, taxes are charged as the interest is paid out. In this case, merely deferring taxes—not avoiding them or managing to get a lower tax rate—gives you 11 percent more after-tax earnings.

Then, of course, there is tax exemption. By custom, the interest on bonds issued by state and local governments is not taxed by the feds. Why would anyone ever buy a bond paying taxable interest when the tax-free kind could be had instead? Taxable bonds pay higher yields. If a very safe corporate bond (say, that Exxon bond again) is yielding 10 percent, an equivalently safe bond with the same redemption date issued by the state of California may yield only 7.5 or 8 percent. More about this in a following chapter.

Some not-so-unimportant side points: Bonds issued by other states are typically taxed by state and local authorities. Such taxes mount up. For example, a New York City resident who owns a tax-exempt bond issued in Florida or Alaska or New Mexico could find that as much as 18 percent of the interest was taxed away. Note, too, that interest paid on federal government bonds is subject to federal income tax, but not to state or local tax. This can be important for residents of high tax states,* particularly when they are choosing between U. S. Treasury securities and equivalently safe (but state-taxable) privately issued investments.

Another reason to hate inflation. . . .

Everybody knows inflation is bad for children and other living things. But lest you ignore the subtler consequences for not-so-conservative investors, ponder this dismal example. Suppose inflation is running at a steady 10 percent a year and the interest rate on a bond due to be redeemed in twenty years is 15 percent. And suppose you invest $1,000 in one of the bonds, then spend the $150 interest earned each year. At the end of the twenty years, you'll get back your $1,000 principal all right. But over the life of the bond, the buying power of your nest egg will have been cut by 85 percent!

That may be all right for the very old or the very ill, who aren't worrying much about how well they'll be living in 2005. But for the rest of us, the only way to stay even with inflation in the long run is to count a portion of the interest paid in inflationary times as a return of principal. In this example, that would mean saving and reinvesting the first 10 percent ($100) of each 15 percent interest payment.

Seem obvious? Apparently it wasn't so obvious to thousands of savers in the inflationary 1970s, who spent their interest earnings and watched the real value of the principal erode. And it still isn't obvious to the U. S. Congress, which continues to tax interest payments as if every penny were truly income.

Penny-wise sometimes means pound-wise, too. . . .

In the hypothetical world of Economics 101, a world of certain information and easy communication, it would be a snap to choose among

---

*Such as Delaware, Iowa, Minnesota, New York, and Vermont, which have maximum income tax rates in excess of 12 percent.

investments. Bonds issued by the Fly-By-Nyte Venetian Blind and Airline Company would certainly pay a higher rate of interest than, say, the U. S. government. But borrowers offering equivalence in safety, maturity, and the like to lenders would be forced to pay equivalent interest. If Fly-By-Nyte tried to sell bonds at 15 percent while its competitor, Air Chance, was offering 15.5 percent, it would be unable to attract any buyers.

In this world, however, it is unrealistic to rely on competition to maintain the balance. Better packaging, better advertising, or smarter selling can catch a lazy or unwary saver on the short end of the interest stick. Is it likely to matter very much? Much depends, no surprise, on the amount of money and the length of time involved. If you are setting aside $1,000 for this summer's vacation, half a percentage point of difference between competing money market funds would probably mean only $5–$10 more or less in interest earnings. Chances are, switching funds from account to account to get the best deal wouldn't be worth the hassle.

Consider, by contrast, a choice between two retirement accounts in which one consistently pays 9 percent interest, the other 9.5 percent. Deposit $2,000 each year in the 9 percent account and after thirty years you'll end up with $297,150. But deposit the same $2,000 a year for the same thirty years in the 9.5 percent account, and you'll have $327,816. The reward for working a little harder to get the best rate: $30,666!

The moral, of course, is to be discriminating with both time and money. It doesn't pay to waste days to earn pennies. But in the few, very large investment decisions most of us make, shopping around can make a very big difference.

2

INSTANT ACCESS

IT'S GREAT TO lock up cash for the kids' medical school tuition, or that new house with a really good kitchen, or maybe retirement in Tahiti. But the grocer, dry cleaner, and telephone company, alas, come first. And before investing in longer-term, higher-yield investments, it's important to set aside enough to cover day-to-day bills. Where to put it depends on how much you value convenience, safety, and predictability. Consider the options.

Bank Savings Accounts

Bankers love 'em. But what's best for bankers is not necessarily best for savers. In this case, in fact, it's the worst.

Regular savings accounts come in "passbook" form, or the newer "statement" form, in which deposits, withdrawals, and interest are reported periodically by written statement. Generally there is no minimum balance required.* There is generally no limit on the size or number of transactions possible each month. Though they are not legally obliged to do so, banks always allow withdrawals on demand. And at all but a few state-insured savings institutions, the principal is guaranteed up to $100,000 by a federally backed insurance corporation.

---

* Don't take this one for granted. Some banks suspend all interest payments when accounts fall below a specified minimum. Some even deduct a monthly service charge!

Now for the bad news. Day-to-day savings accounts usually pay only 5.5 percent interest. That is currently a bit below the yield typically paid on other, safe, easily accessible forms of savings, and far below the return possible, if and when inflation rears its destructive head. Besides, a savings account is a very inconvenient way to store cash, since it is not possible to write checks on the balance.

Why, then, do Americans keep more than $200 billion in passbook accounts? Partially it's inertia; more often it's ignorance. **Millions of savings accounts are owned by people who are frightened or confused by financial matters.** Most banks stopped advertising day-to-day savings long ago because they don't want new business: small, active savings accounts are money-losers, in spite of the low interest they pay. But by the same token, banks are not going out of their way to inform customers with ten or twenty thousand dollars gathering dust in passbook accounts that they could earn much more by transferring their funds.

Are savings accounts right for anyone? They are nice for teaching kids about money and thrift. But that's about it.

Traveler's Checks

Traveler's checks don't, of course, pay interest. Their liquidity, however, can make them extremely useful for people who must fly to Cincinnati on two hours' notice, or people who develop sudden urges to make large purchases on Sunday evening. Merchants who would never consider taking your personal check—and who are reluctant to pay the commission on credit card transactions—will often accept traveler's checks.

A few caveats. Since the companies that issue traveler's checks are naturally eager to hold your money interest-free as long as possible, checks don't have expiration dates. But it can still be mighty hard to replace a five-year-old check if you lose one. **If you make a practice of putting extra checks in a desk drawer for a rainy day, it is absolutely necessary to keep up-to-date records of their serial numbers in some other place.** Otherwise the checks are no more secure than cash.

American Express and the big bank issuers usually charge a fee for traveler's checks, typically one percent of their face value. Lesser-known issuers often waive any fee, earning their profit solely from the interest your money earns on their behalf until you cash the checks. "Brand name" companies justify the fee by arguing their checks are easier to cash and easier to replace if stolen. In truth, **virtually any traveler's check is easy**

to cash and easy to replace in the United States, Europe, Japan, and other heavily traveled countries. If you are using checks to go somewhere else—and have the time to shop around—it's worth inquiring about the arrangements for getting replacements. Chances are, brand ''X'' will do very nicely.

Ordinary Checking Accounts Vs. NOW Accounts

Most banks and savings and loan associations offer NOW (short for ''negotiated order of withdrawal''; you didn't really want to know, did you?) accounts as an alternative to ordinary checking. NOW accounts typically pay 5.25 percent interest; ordinary checking accounts pay no interest at all. But don't jump to conclusions. There may still be reasons for preferring the no-interest variety.

Both regular checking and NOW accounts permit you to write as many checks as you like for sums as small as you like. Both are federally insured up to $100,000. Why, then, would anyone opt for the no-interest alternative? Although there is no law setting minimum or maximum fees on either type of account, the charges for maintaining an ordinary checking account are usually smaller. Banks lose money on every deposit or withdrawal you make—it costs ten to thirty cents to process a check—but count on making it back on the interest they earn loaning out your money.

To make up for the additional cost of providing NOW accounts, banks either set high minimum balances (two to three thousand dollars is typical) or levy higher charges on individual transactions. Then, too, NOW accounts may not include services thrown in free to other depositors. Some banks, for example, waive annual fees for credit cards for customers who maintain regular checking accounts; others provide free checks imprinted with the Mona Lisa or the White House, or perhaps even your address.

Which form of checking is right for you? When banks and savings and loan associations are competing hard for new business, they sometimes offer NOW accounts at terms so advantageous that virtually everyone would be better off with one. **Typically, though, NOW accounts make sense only for individuals who need to keep several thousand dollars on hand.** Others lose more in monthly charges than they make back in interest. The only way to find out for sure, though, is to comparison-shop.

9

Money Market Funds Vs. Bank Money Market Accounts

First some definitions. As far as the government is concerned, a money market fund is a mutual fund, much like a stock market mutual fund. Only instead of investing in stocks or bonds on your behalf, a money market fund lends your cash for short periods to the U. S. Treasury, big banks, big companies, or sometimes even foreign governments. The interest the fund collects on these loans is then paid out as "dividends" to the depositors, who are technically "shareholders" in the fund. MM funds are regulated by the Securities and Exchange Commission. There are over one hundred money market funds that welcome investments from individuals. Typically, they do business entirely by mail and telephone.

A money market account is an account in a bank, savings and loan, or credit union. The money is not invested in any special place; it becomes part of the bank's assets, to be used for everything from car loans to loans to the Rio de Janeiro Electric Company. Unlike MM funds, banks are not obligated to pay out all the interest (after expenses) that they earn. But they must post the rate they intend to pay, month by month.

Minimum deposit. Most funds insist on a minimum initial deposit of $1,000, and minimum subsequent deposits of $100. There are no fixed rules, however. A few demand as much as $20,000 in order to keep out the riffraff. The government regulation requiring a minimum balance in MM accounts was eliminated in January. But in the world of personal finance, free lunches are few and far between. Most banks continue to require some minimum in order to earn the posted interest rate. Typically, that minimum is $2,500. But it may pay to shop around.

Interest. Since MM funds pay out what they earn (after expenses), the yields are determined by the interest they receive lending money in multi-million-dollar chunks. Banks, by contrast, pay what they wish to pay, which is partially related to what they can earn by relending the money, partially to how much they want your business. When banks were first permitted to create MM accounts in 1982, they promoted them by offering very high rates, guaranteed for one month at a time. The promotions worked very well, drawing hundreds of billions in deposits—some of it from the older MM funds. Now they pay what they think they must to remain competitive, which on average turns out to be about the same rate as MM funds.

Note, too, that many banks have a two-tier system for setting interest. Large accounts—sometimes $10,000, sometimes $25,000—pay more than small accounts. Again, there are no government rules. **As long as the rates are posted, banks can pay whatever they like.**

Access. MM funds give you a number of ways to obtain your money—technically, to cash in your shares—very quickly. They provide an unlimited number of checks that work just like bank checks. Typically, though, they must be written for sums greater than $500. Most also give you even faster access by telephone: you call a toll-free number and they wire the requested amount to any bank you designate in advance. Money transferred this way is immediately available from your bank account as cash.

The government no longer limits the number of checks that can be written on MM accounts. And there never has been a restriction on the minimum size of checks on these accounts. But many banks have not dropped the old three-check-a-month rule because they want to discourage use of MM accounts for routine bill paying. If frequency of checkwriting is important to you, shop around for the best deal. Many banks also have arrangements permitting you to transfer funds from an MM account to an ordinary checking account by telephone or by automated teller machine.

Safety. Because it's more straightforward, let's deal with money market accounts first. **Like other deposits in banks and savings and loans, MM accounts are insured up to $100,000 by a government agency.** Even if the bank fails, or the cashier runs off to Brazil with the contents of the vault, your money is safe.

The failure of a number of federally insured banks in recent years has led many people to question the security of deposit insurance. It's true that if several hundred banks all collapsed at once, the two federal insurance agencies (FDIC for banks, FSLIC for savings and loans) wouldn't have sufficient cash in reserve to cover every claim. But such a calamity is very unlikely, even in the event of a 1930s-severity depression. And in any case the government would hardly consider letting small depositors bear the burden. Just five years ago Congress pledged to back federal deposit insurance to the hilt, no matter how big the hit. **The bottom line: if an account is insured by FDIC or FSLIC it's very, very safe.**

Want to be extra sure that your bank is indeed covered? Ask the Federal Deposit Insurance Corporation (202) 393–8400. For savings and loans, ask the Federal Home Loan Bank Board (202) 377–6000.

The money you put in an MM fund is not insured. That doesn't mean, though, that it is in much jeopardy. Funds use your money to buy "certificates of deposit"—in effect, to make loans to big banks, companies, and countries. Even if one of these borrowers went broke, it wouldn't have

UNINSURED BANKS

Two years ago, thousands of depositors found out the hard way that not every bank in America carries federal insurance. Very little money was actually lost by depositors during the crises in Ohio and Maryland. But the two cases should be sufficient warning: No state or private bank insurance system, no matter how well run, has the financial strength to withstand the highly publicized failure of one of its members.

State-insured banks in North Carolina, Massachusetts, and Pennsylvania seem to have gotten the message. By the time you read this, most will have either converted to federal insurance or merged with existing federally insured banks. But this, alas, is not the end of the story. A number of other states tolerate the presence of so-called "industrial banks," which accept consumer deposits. Some are well managed, some aren't. But don't take a chance. If your bank isn't federally insured, move your money to a bank that is. If you aren't sure whether your bank is federally insured, ask, or telephone the federal insurance agencies.

much impact on the value of your shares because no single borrower (except the U. S. government) is ever entrusted with more than a few percentage points of the fund's total assets.

There is another unlikely way you could be hurt. Suppose there was some sort of panic that led everyone to try to withdraw their money (cash in their shares) at the same time. The fund managers might have difficulty selling the fund's assets, and thus would not be able to pay you for days or weeks.

Taken in perspective, the riskiest money market funds just aren't very risky. **Hundreds of billions of dollars have been put in their charge, and nobody has ever lost a cent.** But if you're the type who checks the locks on the front door at least twice before going to bed, you might opt for one of the funds that invests solely in U. S. Treasury securities or one that backs its investments with insurance from a private insurance company (see the end of the chapter for a few suggestions). The feds can't go broke; nor, in the unlikely occurrence of a financial panic, would MM funds have trouble turning Treasury bills into cash. Then, of course, there's the alternative of sticking with a government-insured bank money market account.

The Credit Union Option

For an institution so pervasive, surprisingly few people know what credit unions are or how they operate. Credit unions are cooperatives that take deposits and make small loans, like savings and loan associations. They are usually organized among the employees of a corporation or government agency. In theory they are controlled by the depositors; in practice they are run by committees of volunteers, plus paid employees. About half the 20,000 credit unions are chartered, regulated, and insured (to $100,000 per account) by federal agencies. The other half are directed by the states. Stick with the ones that are federally insured. If you aren't sure, ask.

What does all this have to do with "instant access" accounts? Federally chartered credit unions (and also most state-chartered ones) can give depositors any terms they please on any sort of account they choose to offer. Smaller credit unions—those with deposits under $5 million—usually offer only passbook-type, day-to-day savings accounts. They typically pay a percentage point or two more interest than banks. But the larger ones usually offer money market accounts, too.

Since there are no fixed rules, and since no one keeps up-to-date information on credit union accounts, it is hard to compare them with bank accounts. There are a few general points of comparison, though. In urban areas where banks are slugging hot and heavy for consumer deposits, credit unions aren't likely to be able to provide better interest rates. **In smaller cities with only one or two banks, though, the credit union at a local factory may be very competitive indeed.** In any case, it never hurts to find out.

Selected Money Market Funds

If you're looking for a money market fund, this very abbreviated list offers a head start in selecting the right one for you. **The fact that a fund is not on this list doesn't mean it is somehow inferior.** The idea is simply to offer a choice of larger funds that might suit your special needs. Almost all, as noted, have toll-free numbers so that you can obtain more information for the price of a local phone call. If the toll-free number does not work from where you live, the funds will usually accept collect calls.

Funds with low minimum investments. Most funds require an initial deposit of $1,000. A few require as much as $20,000. But the ones below can be opened with as little as $500:

> AARP U. S. Government Money Market Trust
> (800) 245–4770–outside Pennsylvania
> (412) 392–6300

> Daily Cash Accumulation
> (800) 525–9310

> Franklin Group Money Funds
> (800) 632–2180

Funds with no minimums on check withdrawals. Most funds require checks to be written for $500 or more, so you will not burden them with check-clearing costs. But, at the time this guide was going to press, at least one money market fund had decided to permit checkwriting without any minimum. The one big catch: the minimum investment is $10,000.

> Fidelity Daily Income Trust
> (800) 544–6666—outside Massachusetts
> (617) 523–1919

Another fund has a similar policy, but one based on a more flexible formula. It permits unlimited free checking for sums above $300 and limited, free checking for smaller amounts. If, for example, you maintain a balance of $5,000, you are permitted to write five free checks a month. Additional checks cost 30 cents.

> Liquid Green Trust
> (800) 862–7283—outside Indiana
> (317) 634–3300

Funds with low-cost exchange privileges. Many money market funds are owned by investment companies that also run mutual funds investing in stocks, corporate bonds, and the like. They usually permit you to transfer cash from your money market fund to other investments simply by tele-phoning—and paying a small charge, usually $5. You may never use the exchange privilege, but it's handy to have the option.

> Dreyfus Money Market Funds
> (800) 645–6561—outside New York City
> (718) 895–1206

Fidelity Group Money Market Funds
(800) 225–6190—outside Massachusetts
(617) 523–1919

Rowe Price Group Money Market Funds
(800) 638–5660—outside Maryland
(301) 547–2308

Scudder Group Money Market Funds
(800) 225–2470—outside Massachusetts
(617) 482–3990

Tax-exempt funds. The dividend income on regular money market funds is fully taxable. But some funds buy only tax-exempt securities issued by state and local governments and other qualifying agencies. The dividends they pay are not taxed by Uncle Sam. Before you leap, though, consider two important points. First, tax-exempt funds have very low yields, typically just about half the yield of regular funds. Unless you have a taxable family income exceeding $80,000, and are thus in a high tax bracket, they aren't for you. Second, dividends from these funds are usually taxed by the state you live in. In a high-tax state like New York or Minnesota, that could make a big difference.

Calvert Tax-Free Reserves Money Market
(800) 368–2748—outside the District of Columbia
(301) 951–4800

Dreyfus Tax-Exempt Money Market Fund
(800) 645–6561—outside New York
(718) 895–1206

Franklin Tax-Free Income Fund
(800) 632–2180

Lexington Tax-Free Daily Income Fund
(800) 526–0057

Nuveen Tax-Exempt Money Fund
(800) 621–2431—outside New York
(212) 668–9500

Vanguard Municipal Bond Fund Money Market Portfolio
(800) 662–7447

U. S. government-backed securities only. The safety-conscious investor (who nonetheless prefers to forego the absolute safety of a government-insured bank account) can choose a fund that buys only federal or federally backed securities. Remember, there is a price for this extra margin of safety: these funds usually pay about half a percentage point less than funds with the freedom to buy bank certificates of deposit or loan money to corporations.

Capital Preservation Fund
(800) 227–8380—outside California
(800) 982–6150—in California

Dreyfus Money Market Instruments—Government
(800) 645–6561—outside New York
(212) 895–1206

First Variable Rate Fund for Government Income
(800) 368–2748—outside Maryland
(301) 951–4820

Scudder Government Money Fund
(800) 225–2470—outside Massachusetts
(617) 482–3990

Vanguard Money Market Trust Federal
(800) 662–7447

Privately insured funds. An alternative to a fund that buys only government securities is one that insures its portfolio of privately issued securities through an insurance company. If one of the securities owned by the fund defaults on interest or principal, the insurance company pays. Not quite as safe as securities backed by the credit of the U. S. government, but the interest yields should average a little higher.

Vanguard Insured Money Market Portfolio
(800) 662–7447

Selected Bank
Money Market Accounts

Banks have different strategies for getting and keeping money market accounts—free checking, automated teller access, and the like. These offer what many depositors want most: very high interest rates. The list is surely not complete. For an up-to-the-minute survey of top-paying banks, buy a copy of *Barron's Financial Weekly* on the newsstand. The magazine's Market Week section has a list of the banks that paid the highest rates the previous week. Or if you are really serious about maximizing your return, subscribe to the source of *Barron's* reports, a weekly publication called *Hundred Highest Yields*, (800) 327–7717.

A minor drawback to setting up accounts at the S&L's below is that you must bank by mail and/or toll-free telephone. At very least, though, they offer a handy yardstick by which to compare the yields on banks paid near your home.

Audubon Federal Savings and Loan
Metairie, Louisiana
(504) 454–5300

Capitol Bank and Trust
Boston, Massachusetts
(617) 723–5300

Continental Savings Association
Angleton, Texas
(800) 231–1073

Crescent Federal Savings Bank
New Orleans, Louisiana
(800) 223–9617

Guaranty Federal Savings
San Antonio, Texas
(512) 656–0202

OBA Federal Savings and Loan
Washington, D.C.
(202) 628–7300

Virginia Beach Federal
Virginia Beach, Virginia
(800) 368–3090

Western Savings
Gatesville, Texas
(800) 231–4212

TIPS

$ If you keep more than $500 in a passbook savings account, run, do not walk, to the nearest bank or money market fund and transfer the money to an account that pays higher interest.

$ For most investors seeking instant access, bank money market accounts have the edge over money market funds. The accounts are slightly more secure, yet pay about the same interest.

$ At most banks, NOW accounts are a better deal than ordinary checking for people who average more than a $2,000 balance. The interest earned on large NOW balances typically exceeds the extra monthly charges assessed on NOW accounts.

$ There are no government rules limiting interest on money market accounts. As a result, interest rates vary widely. The only way to be sure you're getting a good deal is to shop around.

PLAYING FOR MORE TIME

MONEY MARKET FUNDS and bank accounts offer immediate access to your cash, plus protection of capital. But, typically, the interest return is low. By contrast, bonds, Ginnie Mae pass-through certificates, and other long-term fixed-income securities pay a higher interest return, but exact a penalty should you need the cash in a hurry (see Chapter 4). Worse, their value can fall sharply if interest rates rise.

Which to choose? One way to go is to mix your assets—long-term for high income, short-term for liquidity and safety. The other way to compromise is to buy securities that mature in, say, six months to five years. **These intermediate-term assets generally pay more interest than the money market accounts, yet lose less value than long-term bonds when interest rates rise.** By the same token, they do not permit you to lock in high yields for very long periods. Consider some of the options.

U. S. Savings Bonds

Just a few years ago the savings bond program was a national disgrace, using patriotism to con low-income families into lending money to Washington at below-market interest rates. All that has changed. **The new series EE savings bonds provide a very decent means of earning competitive interest rates and preserving capital.**

Here's how the new system now works. You buy an EE bond in multiples of $25 at most banks. Or, if your employer is in the program, you can buy bonds directly through payroll deductions. Provided you hold on to the bonds for at least five years, you earn interest equal to 85 percent of the average yield on five-year Treasury notes over the period. If by chance the interest rate calculated by this formula is below 7.5 percent, the government pays a minimum 7.5 percent anyway*. So if the average Treasury note rate over five years was, say, 11 percent, you would receive 9.35 percent. If, however, the average Treasury note rate was just 6 percent, you would receive the 7.5 percent minimum. Savings bonds may be redeemed for full investment value, plus earned interest, anytime between the fifth and the tenth year.

Ponder the advantages. Like all government bonds, the principal and interest are default-proof. Like all government bonds, interest is free from state or local taxes. But unlike other bonds, government-issue or not, there is no market risk. **Uncle Sam will redeem a savings bond for the full value of the principal before the redemption date, no matter what happens to market interest rates.** And, as a bonus, federal taxes on the interest are deferred until you cash in the bond.

There is one serious catch, though. For the first six months after purchase, there is no way to redeem a savings bond. Between the sixth month and twelfth month a savings bond can be converted back to cash at virtually any bank, but you receive only 5.5 percent interest. Hold the bond longer, and the rate gradually increases. Between one and two years, it pays 6 percent; two to three, 6.5 percent; three to four, 7 percent; four to five, 7.5 percent.

Savings bonds, then, aren't meant for people who might need the money back within six months. And they are a dubious investment for people who are likely to need the money within five years. But for longer-term savers savings bonds can be a nice way to earn a fairly high, tax-deferred yield with no risk of principal.

The real competition to savings bonds is single-premium deferred annuities (see Chapter 5). Annuities, too, preserve principal and defer taxes—and they are apt to pay a somewhat higher interest rate than savings bonds. Their only disadvantages: most annuity plans require a minimum investment of $5,000; annuities are not backed by the government; and any withdrawal of interest before the tenth year is subject to a special federal penalty tax on top of regular income taxes.

---

*As *Where to Put Your Money 1987* was going to press, there were rumors of reduction in the guaranteed minimum rate, most likely to 6 percent. At that rate, bonds would still be a good deal but not the steal they were at 7.5 percent.

Treasury Bills and Notes

The terminology can be confusing, but the ideas are simple. **A Treasury bill is an interest-paying security issued by the U. S. government that matures in one year or less.** In fact, T-bills are issued in just four maturities: ninety-one days, six months, nine months, and one year. If, for some reason, you wanted a T-bill that matured in a specific week, you could always buy an old one through a bank or broker. T-bills come in face values of $10,000.

A Treasury note is a U. S. government security with a face value of $1,000 that matures between one and ten years. While three- and six-month T-bills are auctioned off each week, there are fewer opportunities to buy T-notes direct from Uncle Sam. Two-year notes are auctioned once a month; longer-term notes of varying maturities are auctioned quarterly. Notes, new and "seasoned," are available through banks and brokers.

Both the principal and interest on all Treasury securities are guaranteed against default. Until quite recently, most notes were sold in "bearer" form. The certificate of ownership had no name on it; interest, payable semiannually, could be collected by clipping a coupon and then redeeming it at a commercial bank or a branch of the Federal Reserve Bank system. Old bearer notes are still around. But since January 1983 all notes have been issued in "registered" form. The note has the owner's name and Social Security number written on it, and semiannual interest is paid automatically by check.

T-bills, by contrast, are sold in "discount" form. When you buy a newly issued bill direct from the Federal Reserve, you pay the full $10,000 face value. The Federal Reserve then immediately returns a smaller check to you, prepaying the interest the T-bill will earn over its short life. Should you wish to sell the T-bill through a broker before it matures, you'll receive less than $10,000—the difference being the interest on the T-bill the buyer is to get. If you hold the T-bill to maturity, of course, you'll receive the $10,000 back from the Federal Reserve.

Buying a T-bill or T-note. The simplest way to buy 'em or sell 'em is through a bank or broker. **If you are willing to put in a little effort, though, you can save $15–$25 per transaction by purchasing them direct from branches of the Federal Reserve.** The New York Federal Reserve has a seven-day, twenty-four-hour phone service providing details for individual purchasers. Call (212) 791–5823. Alternatively you can write to: Bureau of Public Debt, Dept. F, Washington, DC 20226.

For T-bill information, write for "Basic Information on Treasury Bills" to: Federal Reserve Bank of New York, 33 Liberty Street, New York, NY 10045.

Are T-bills or T-notes right for you? Before the invention of money market funds, T-bills were one of the few ways for small investors to obtain competitive rates of interest on short-term investments. **Today they are probably more trouble than they are worth.** Money market bank accounts are guaranteed by the federal government and typically pay about the same interest rate. Banks also issue government-guaranteed certificates of deposit that pay about the same interest rate as T-notes. But T-notes can be sold through brokers without any interest penalty. **Buy T-notes for maximum liquidity, bank CDs for maximum convenience.**

Bank Savings Certificates (Certificates of Deposit)

Until October 1983 the federal government enforced an elaborate set of rules about what terms banks and savings and loan associations could offer for insured deposits of varying lengths. But the feds have swept away most of those regulations. Now it is largely up to the banks—or rather, to competition between banks and other borrowers—to set the terms.

First, what is left of the rules? If you still have a government-insured savings certificate from before October 1983, the old rules apply: read the fine print. **For new, insured certificates there is no longer any government regulation on interest rates, minimum deposits, or penalties for withdrawal before the certificate expires.**

What rates and terms, then, are you likely to receive? Much depends on how much the banks (and, of course, S&Ls) want your money. Local rate wars may break out periodically, triggered by banks eager to expand their deposits. So, most likely, there will be periodic opportunities to earn extremely high interest for a few months at a time. The idea, from the bank's point of view, is that you'll leave the money on deposit after the party's over. Typically, though, one can expect rates for deposits over $1,000 to more or less track the yields on U. S. Treasury bills and notes.

Are savings certificates right for you? Compare them to bank money market accounts or money market funds. **Unless you have a very large sum to invest, the slightly higher interest rate to be earned on certificates maturing in a year or less is not likely to outweigh the inconvenience of lack of access.** A bank might, of course, offer you a very special rate for a short time. But before you bite, do the interest arithmetic for yourself.

What about longer-term certificates maturing, say, in one to eight years? Here the choices get trickier. Compare them first to Treasury notes of equivalent term. Interest on T-notes is free of state or local tax, and you can sell the T-notes before maturity through a broker without paying an interest penalty. On the other hand, the market value of a five-year T-note can fall considerably if interest rates rise. The most you can lose on a savings certificate is ninety days' interest.

It is also smart to compare the intermediate-term certificate with a longer-term investment like a Treasury bond. If the interest rate on, say, a ten-year bond is considerably higher than the rate on a five-year savings certificate, lock in the higher yield with a portion of your savings.

One last point. Many banks are offering the alternative of variable rates on savings certificates maturing in two or more years. The variable rate is usually a lower rate, keyed to the Treasury bill rate. Variable-rate certificates might be worth the sacrifice for very conservative investors if ordinary fixed-return bank certificates truly locked you in to a fixed interest rate to maturity. In fact, you can always bail out of a fixed-rate certificate by paying the interest penalty. The bottom line: variable-rate certificates are generally losers.

Shopping for CDs

Is the Last Interstate Bank offering 7.10 percent interest on a CD paying a higher rate than the Confederated Federated Bank offering 7.00 percent? Not necessarily. Everything depends on how frequently each bank compounds interest.

Say Last Interstate has a policy of crediting interest to your account just once a year. Invest $10,000 in the Last Interstate one-year CD, and you'll end up with $10,710.

Now assume that Confederated Federated compounds interest monthly: each month, it takes the few dollars of interest you've earned and adds it to the principal. That, in effect, allows you to earn interest on your interest as the year goes along. Twelve months after the initial $10,000 deposit, you'll have $10,723, or $13 more than you would earn from Last Interstate.

How, then, to compare interest rates on CDs? **Ask the bank what "effective annual yield" it pays.** Banks that don't know usually have something to hide. Or use the table below.

COMPOUNDED	**A CD Paying This Rate:**					
	6%	7%	8%	9%	10%	11%
	has an EFFECTIVE ANNUAL YIELD of:					
annually	6.000	7.000	8.000	9.000	10.000	11.000
quarterly	6.136	7.186	8.243	9.308	10.381	11.462
monthly	6.168	7.229	8.300	9.381	10.471	11.572
weekly	6.180	7.246	8.322	9.409	10.507	11.615
daily	6.183	7.250	8.328	9.416	10.516	11.626

Save for variations in the penalties charged for premature withdrawal, one federally insured bank CD is pretty much like any other. That makes it possible to shop by telephone, comparing effective annual yields on CDs of different maturities. The following banks have a policy of paying very high rates. Note, however, that some may require substantial minimum deposits—$10,000 or even $25,000—to get the best rates offered.

Call banks in your own area for comparison. Or check the listings of top savings deposit yields in the Market Week section of *Barron's Financial Weekly*, available on newsstands.

Alamo Savings
San Antonio, Texas
(512) 828–7171

Frontier Savings
Las Vegas, Nevada
(702) 796–4400

Laurel Savings
Laurel, Maryland
(301) 725–2552

Western Gulf Savings
Bay City, Texas
(409) 245–5751

Western Savings
Gatesville, Texas
(817) 865–7205

Floating-Rate Notes

A lot of companies borrow money by selling what is called "commercial paper"—notes due in weeks or months that pay a somewhat higher rate than Treasury bills or notes of comparable maturity. The minimum investment is usually very large—$50,000 or more—making commercial paper inaccessible to most individuals. But a few, notably the "holding company" parents of big banks, offer a more accessible variation.

Floating-rate notes with a face value of $1,000 have been issued with maturities as long as ten years. Rather than paying a fixed-coupon interest rate, the semiannual payment is keyed to current short-term interest rates. The key is usually the rate paid on six-month Treasury bills or on certificates of deposit at large banks, plus some premium. Citicorp (the parent company of Citibank), for example, has issued floating-rate notes paying 1.05 percentage points more than the T-bill rate, with a minimum of 6 percent no matter how low the T-bill goes.

Floating-rate notes issued by corporations will always pay a bit more than T-bills, and are more convenient to own since they need not be renewed every six months. Like T-bills or short-term negotiable savings certificates, floating notes won't decline very much in value when interest rates rise. But there are drawbacks, too. While floating notes are easy enough to buy or sell through a broker, the market is not nearly as liquid as the market for Treasury securities. As a result, you are likely to lose more of their value—probably a few percentage points—should you need to dispose of them quickly.

Remember, too, that floating-rate issues are no more secure than the company that backs them. That, in all likelihood, is very secure indeed, since the issuers are large, successful corporations. But don't draw too much comfort from the fact that the issuer happens to be a bank: **notes are not bank deposits, and are thus not guaranteed by the federal government.**

Intermediate-Term Bond Funds

The rules are pretty much the same for intermediate-term bond funds as they are for short-term money market funds on the one hand, or long-term bond funds on the other. Here you pay (a minimum of $1,000) into a fund that uses the cash to buy bonds with maturities of less (often considerably less) than ten years. Some funds invest only in government-insured bonds, some only in tax-exempt bonds. All pay out the interest to shareholders, less a fee to cover expenses and profit. Funds allow you to sell back your shares for their underlying value whenever you choose.

The big advantages of a bond fund are convenience and diversification. They do the work, comparing the return and safety of various securities. They automatically reinvest your interest, unless you specifically request that it be paid to you in cash. Many permit you to write checks (greater than $500) against the value of your shares. And by diversifying into dozens of different securities, funds offer greater safety than an individual could achieve by buying a single issue of uninsured corporate bonds.

The disadvantage is cost. It is possible to avoid all fees for buying or selling shares by sticking with ''no-load'' funds. But there is no way to avoid paying for the service: the return on a no-load bond fund will be about half a percentage point less than you could earn by purchasing the securities in the fund's portfolio.

On balance, intermediate-term funds can be a very competitive alternative to savings bonds or savings certificates. **You might even consider using one as a less conservative alternative to a money market fund or bank money market account (see Chapter 2).** Remember, though, that the value of shares in an intermediate-term fund will vary as interest rates rise or fall.

These funds pay relatively high rates because they invest in nonguaranteed corporate bonds:

Fidelity Thrift Trust
(800) 544–6666—outside Massachusetts
(617) 523–1919

Safeco Special Bond Fund
(800) 426–6730—outside Washington State
(800) 562–6810—in Washington State

Vanguard Short Term Bond Portfolio
(800) 662–7447

This fund pays lower rates because it invests only in Treasury securities:

Capital Preservation Treasury Note Trust
(800) 472–3389—outside California
(800) 982–6150—in California

These funds pay still lower rates because the income, from intermediate-term municipal bonds, is exempt from federal taxes:

Scudder Tax-Free Target Fund
(800) 225–2470

Vanguard Intermediate-Term Municipal Bond Fund
(800) 662–7447

TIPS

$ Securities maturing in one to ten years yield less interest than long-term securities. But they appeal to conservative savers because there is less risk of capital loss.

$ A bank savings certificate (also known as a certificate of deposit) is a solid, conservative investment because it is government-insured and can be cashed in for a small interest penalty. But you must shop around to get the best deal.

$ U. S. savings bonds pay competitively high interest and can be a real buy for savers with only a few hundred dollars to put away. But to enjoy the full benefit, you must hold savings bonds for at least five years.

$ Treasury bills and notes are as solid as Fort Knox. For those who value convenience, though, a bank money market account is likely to be a better deal than a T-bill maturing in less than a year.

$ Intermediate-term bond funds combine convenience and competitive yield. Consider a fund as an alternative to a money market account.

4

LOCKING IN YIELD

BACK IN THE late fifties and early sixties, investors found corporate bonds paying 4–5 percent interest almost irresistible. The chance of a lifetime, many thought, to lock in record-high interest rates for decades to come. Hardly anyone, of course, had an inkling of the great inflation to come, or its effect on interest rates and bond values. Most of those original investors, older and possibly wiser, sold their bonds long ago for a fraction of what they had paid.

Why, you might ask, begin a chapter on long-term investment with memories of investment folly? Why not begin with happy stories about the folks who bought high-quality bonds paying 18 percent a few years ago, bonds that are now worth 30–40 percent more than their initial cost? Because in a time when interest rates can fluctuate dramatically, any investment in long-term, fixed-return securities is risky. It may still make sense for conservative investors, tempted by high yields, to buy some of the securities discussed here. **But unless you are prepared to lose a lot of money, their place in your "portfolio" should be relatively modest.**

U. S. Treasury Bonds

The federal government is the single largest issuer of bonds; maturities range from five to twenty years. Treasury bonds have a face value of

$1,000. Their market value, however, can be larger or smaller, depending on whether current interest rates are lower or higher than the day the bond was issued. Treasuries pay a fixed return (called the "coupon" rate because the interest is paid to owners of interest coupons clipped from the bonds) twice a year. Treasury bonds may be purchased (or sold) for a small fee through many banks and all stockbrokers.

In most newspapers, listings of Treasury bonds look like this:

Rate	Date	Bid	Ask	Chg	Yield
8¼s	2000–05 May	77.1	77.19	– .31	10.98

Here, the coupon rate (usually followed by the letter "s"; I don't know why either) is 8.25 percent. That means the bond pays $82.50 a year interest on its face value of $1,000.00. At the maturity date, the full $1,000.00 is returned to the owner of the bond. When two maturity dates (2000, 2005) are listed, as above, the government guarantees to redeem the bond at the later date but has the option to redeem it at the earlier one.

The "bid" is the price that dealers will pay for the bond. Note that it is expressed as a percentage of the face value. Just to confuse things, the numbers after the decimal refer to thirty-seconds of a percentage point (in effect, thirty-seconds of $10.00). The bid here is 77¹⁄₃₂, or, translating to dollars, $770.31. The "asked" column tells you what dealers are willing to sell the bond for: 77¹⁹⁄₃₂, or $775.94 (77 x 10, plus ¹⁹⁄₃₂ x 10). The "change" is the change in the bid from the previous day, again in thirty-seconds of a point. Here the change is ³¹⁄₃₂ of a point (in money, $9.69).

The last column gives the annual yield you would earn by purchasing the bond for the ask price and holding it to maturity. Most of the yield comes from the semiannual interest payments. But a little piece of it comes from the bond's gradual gain in value as it goes from the current price of $775.94 to the redemption price of $1,000.00 in the year 2005.

Bonds selling for less than their face value, as in this case, are especially attractive. There is less chance the government will exercise its right to redeem the bond at the earliest possible date—there would be no point, after all, for the government to pay $1,000 for a bond that was worth less than $1,000 on the open market.

Treasury bonds are free from any risk of default. And the market for the bonds is enormous, making it a snap to sell them at a moment's notice. Another plus is that Treasury bonds, like all U. S. government debts, are free of state and local tax. That may not make a giant difference, but it's worth remembering when comparing Treasury bonds with privately issued bonds and other fixed-income securities.

Now the bad news. **Like any long-term fixed-income security, a Treasury bond will lose a lot of value if interest rates rise sharply.** With T-bonds you pay for security against default: yields are usually about one percentage point lower than very high quality corporate bonds with the same maturity. But the benefits of superior liquidity, safety, and partial tax exemption make Treasury bonds the better buy for the most conservative investors.

Other Government Bonds

Government agency bonds. You may have read about "off-budget" government financing, the hidden debt of government agencies other than the Treasury. Over one hundred such issues can be purchased by the public. The most important are bonds from the Federal Home Loan Bank, the Bank for Cooperatives, the Federal Land Bank, and the Federal Intermediate Credit Bank.

Never mind what these agencies do with the money. For our purposes what counts is that, like Treasury bonds, most are guaranteed by the feds. They are better than T-bonds in the sense that they pay about one percentage point higher interest. **But there's a catch. For many agency issues, there are relatively few buyers and sellers.** So the cost of trading—roughly the spread between the bid and asked price—is considerably larger than the cost of buying or selling Treasury bonds. Agency bonds are thus a relatively good buy only if you plan to hold them to maturity. Like T-bonds, they can be purchased from banks or brokers.

International agency bonds. The World Bank, Asian Development Bank, and Interamerican Development Bank are all international agencies that raise private capital to aid development projects in poor countries. That doesn't sound very safe, but it is; their debts are, in effect, guaranteed by the governments of the developed countries. They pay somewhat more interest than Treasury bonds and are somewhat less liquid. All in all, a competitive alternative for investors who would otherwise buy Treasury bonds and hang on to them for several years. International agency bonds can be purchased from brokers.

Corporate Bonds

Hundreds of large corporations raise money by selling long-term bonds. Corporate bonds pay interest twice a year and can be purchased in $1,000 face-value units from brokers. The price of a corporate bond is quoted as a percentage of the $1,000 face value. The pricing system is a bit different (and a bit simpler), though, than the one used for Treasury bonds. Fractions of percentages are listed in eighths, so 68⅞ translated into the actual dollar price of the bond would be $688.88 (68 x 10, plus ⅞ x 10).

Corporate bonds are not guaranteed. **A bond owner's degree of protection against default depends on the financial strength of the corporation and/or the specific backing behind the bonds.** Many airlines, for example, are in relatively poor financial shape. So in order to finance new equipment at reasonably low interest rates, they pledge specific aircraft as collateral. Corporate bonds, like tax-exempt bonds, are rated for safety by Moody's and Standard and Poor's credit services; rating information can be obtained from any broker. For an explanation of the rating systems, see Chapter 5.

Most corporate bonds are bought and sold either through the American Exchange or the New York Exchange, and their prices are listed daily on newspaper financial pages. A typical listing would look like this:

Bonds	Current Yield	Sales in $1,000	High	Low	Last	Net Chge
ATT 13¼ 91	12.5	75	106¼	105⅞	106	−⅛

This AT&T (Ma Bell) bond, due to mature in 1991, pays a coupon interest rate of 13.25 percent, $132.50 annually on the $1,000.00 face value. The current yield (the coupon payment divided by the current market price) is 12.5 percent. Seventy-five bonds changed hands on this particular day, at prices ranging between $1,062.50 and $1,058.88. The last price paid on the trade was $1,060.00. The change in price from the preceding day was just $1.25.

Note, by the way, that the bond is trading above the $1,000 it originally sold for. That puts the current owner at a disadvantage in two ways. First, the bond may contain a "call" provision, permitting AT&T to redeem the bond before maturity for a specific price, perhaps below the $1,060 it is currently selling for. **Always check the call provision in the contract**

31

before buying a bond. Second, it is important to remember that the bond must inevitably decline in value by 1991 since AT&T will redeem it for just $1,000 in that year. So the current yield of 12.5 percent is somewhat greater than the average yield figured to maturity.

Should you buy corporate bonds? Their yield is always higher than Treasury bonds; how much higher depends on the credit rating of the bond. Very secure bonds (like that AT&T bond) typically pay about one percentage point more than T-bonds of the same maturity. **One big disadvantage of most corporates is their lack of liquidity.** With relatively few bonds bought and sold each day, you might have to accept a 2–3 percent loss in order to find a buyer quickly. Another is that interest income on corporates is subject to state and local, as well as federal, tax. Still another disadvantage is complexity. To buy with confidence, you need to know a lot about the backing behind a corporate bond.

The bottom line: conservative investors are better off sticking to bonds with top credit ratings that are selling below face value and are actively traded. A short list of candidates would include the bonds of AT&T, most regional Bell Telephone companies, General Motors Acceptance Corporation, Ford Credit, and Xerox. Better yet, small investors can take advantage of professional management and diversification offered by corporate bond mutual funds and unit trusts. They are discussed next.

Bond Funds and Unit Trusts

Small investors (a) have trouble getting and keeping the attention of a bond broker, (b) are not able to scour the prospectuses of hundreds of bond issues to check credit ratings and call provisions, and (c) are not able to diversify by buying a dozen different issues. That is where funds and unit trusts come in.

A bond fund is what you'd expect: a mutual fund that specializes in buying corporate bonds. In theory, they help guard your capital by selling before interest rates rise and buying before interest rates fall. Whether they succeed in the long run is questionable. But they most certainly do manage to create high-quality, diversified portfolios.

Most bond funds are "open-ended." You buy shares at the underlying asset value (less any commissions), then sell them whenever you want to for the underlying asset value. Many, alas, do charge commissions, or "loads," as high as 8 percent. **Stick with bond funds that charge no load, earning their income from a portion of the interest income generated by the fund.** A very short list of no-load funds:

Calvert Income Portfolio
(800) 368–2748—outside Maryland
(301) 951–4820

Columbia Fixed Income Securities
(800) 547–1037—outside Oregon
(503) 222–3600

Dreyfus A Bond Plus
(800) 645–6561—outside New York
(718) 895–1206

Fidelity Thrift Trust
(800) 544–6666—outside Massachusetts
(617) 523–1919

SteinRoe Managed Bond Fund
(800) 621–0320—outside Illinois
(312) 368–7826

Vanguard Fixed Income—Investment Grade
(800) 662–7447

The alternative to a fund is a corporate bond unit trust. Here a big brokerage house like Merrill Lynch buys several million dollars' worth of bonds, then divides the pie into $1,000 slices. You pay the broker a single fixed premium—typically 3 percent of the value of the units—and in return get a piece of an unchanging (but diversified) portfolio of securities. Should you wish to sell, the broker typically guarantees to buy back your units for the underlying value of the bonds. For a small annual fee, the brokerage house sends you monthly interest checks and keeps records for taxes.

Between the two, a unit trust has the edge for people who are confident they will hold the investment for at least five years. If you aren't so confident but still want to invest in a diversified portfolio of taxable corporate bonds, one of the bond funds makes more sense.

Zero-Coupon Securities

A zero-coupon security is a bond (or, if the issuer is a bank, a certificate of deposit) that does not pay interest semiannually like an ordinary bond. Why, then, would anybody buy one?

"Zeros" sell at enormous discounts from their ultimate redemption value. You earn interest all right, but the interest simply isn't paid until you redeem the bond at maturity. For example, a $1,000 zero-coupon bond that yields the equivalent of 10 percent and matures in twenty years will sell for just $142. The extra $858 paid on redemption represents the twenty years' interest on the $142, plus the interest on the interest! The chart below will give you a feel for the relationship between purchase price, interest rate, and redemption value:

Invest in a zero-coupon bond due to mature in this many years:	If the Bond Earns This Much Interest Annually:					
	7%	8%	9%	10%	11%	12%
	You Must Invest This Much to End Up with $1,000					
10 years	$502.57	$456.39	$414.64	$376.89	$342.73	$311.80
15 years	$356.28	$308.32	$267.00	$231.38	$200.64	$174.11
20 years	$252.57	$208.29	$171.93	$142.05	$117.46	$ 97.22
30 years	$126.93	$ 95.06	$ 71.29	$ 53.54	$ 40.26	$ 30.31

Zero-coupon bonds have been all the rage on Wall Street in recent years, and it's easy to see why. First, they exploit a gimmick; hardheaded types who know all about compound interest are still mesmerized by the idea of investing just $71.29 in a 9 percent zero and getting a whopping $1,000.00 back in thirty years.

But zeros are more than a gimmick. An ordinary fixed-income security like a long-term bond allows you to lock in the annual income, but it doesn't guarantee that you will be able to reinvest the semiannual interest payments at an equivalent interest rate. Zeros give you that second level of protection, locking in both the interest on the initial investment and the interest you will receive on the reinvested income. **Thus a zero-coupon bond tells you exactly how much you'll end up with if you set aside a given amount of cash for a given amount of years.**

Zeros come in four flavors: corporate, tax-exempt, Treasury security, and bank CD. Corporate zeros have been issued by dozens of businesses, most of them very large and very blue chip. Their bigness and blueness should not surprise anyone, for the buyer must put a lot of faith in the credit of the borrower—betting, in effect, that the company will be around in ten, twenty, or thirty years to pay off the accumulated interest and principal. Zero-coupon tax-exempts are zeros issued by municipalities, states, and other agencies entitled to issue tax-exempt bonds.

Treasury security zeros are an investment product invented just a few years ago by big investment banking houses in order to cash in on the craze for zero-coupon securities. An investment company buys a bunch of ordinary long-term Treasury bonds and strips off the coupons that entitle the owner to a fixed amount of interest every six months. It then issues zero-coupon bonds backed by the Treasury coupons, which are held as collateral by a bank. And there you have it: a synthetic zero-coupon bond, with principal and interest backed by Treasury securities nestling in a bank vault. Salomon Brothers calls them CATS (Certificates of Accrual on Treasury Securities); Merrill Lynch calls its version TIGRs (Treasury Investment Growth Receipts). The "felines" have been such a big hit with investors that Uncle Sam decided to get into the act in 1985. The government's version, guaranteed directly by the Treasury, are called STRIPS (Separate Trading of Registered Interest and Principal of Securities). Cute, huh!

A few banks are selling zero-coupon certificates of deposit, either directly to bank customers or through brokerage houses. These CDs are insured to $100,000 like any other federally insured bank account.

Which flavor (if any) is to your taste? The big appeal of zeros is that you know exactly how much you have to put in today in order to end up with $1,000 (or $10,000 or $100,000) when, say, the kids are ready for college. But you pay for that advantage in a number of ways.

First, the effective interest yield on zeros is apt to be a half to a full percentage point lower than on an ordinary bond of equivalent safety and maturity. Second, in all but the case of tax-exempt zeros, you must pay income taxes (at regular, not capital gains, rates) on the interest you earn each year, even though you don't see a penny of the income until the bond matures.

Third, tax-exempt issuers often sabotage the neatest feature of a zero, namely the ability to lock in interest rates. The fine print on the bond contract allows the issuer to redeem the bond early for much less than the final $1,000 redemption value. So if interest rates fall a few years after you buy the bond, the issuer "calls" it back, leaving you with the problem of where to reinvest your money.

What does all that add up to? Much depends on how much interest you are willing to sacrifice in order to lock in rates as tightly as possible. **Taxable zero-coupon securities, particularly Treasury and Treasury-**

backed issues, are a good "buy it and forget it" investment for a tax-deferred Keogh plan or IRA (see Chapter 7). Tax-exempt zeros make marginal sense for conservative high-income investors, providing the issue does not contain a call provision of any sort.

Ginnie Maes

This is a funny sort of security, since it has no fixed life and no fixed yield. But as you shall see, it's a pretty attractive asset for those looking for safe, high, current income. The Government National Mortgage Association, a federal agency, buys government-insured home mortgages from the banks and savings and loan associations that originally lent the money. The agency then packages the mortgages in multimillion-dollar hunks, adds its own guarantee against default, and sells them to big brokerage houses. The brokers, in turn, mark up the package by a few percentage points to make a profit and sell them in $25,000 slices to people like you.

There is a strong resale market for Ginnie Maes, so the same brokers who sell new ones sell "preowned" ones as well. The price of a Ginnie Mae, like a bond, is quoted as a percentage of the face value. Thus a Ginnie Mae selling for 80 would cost 80 percent of $25,000.

If you bought one you would own a tiny fraction of several hundred different home mortgages, with timely payment of interest and principal guaranteed by Uncle Sam. Once a month you would get a check that would represent your share of the mortgage payments, plus your share of any mortgages that were paid off in the previous thirty days.

The mortgages in a "Ginnie Mae pass-through certificate" have an average life of thirty years. But the mortgages automatically come due when the debtor sells the house. So Ginnie Mae certificates typically earn interest for just twelve to fifteen years. The interest income, usually about the same interest as very high-quality corporate bonds, is fully taxable. Each year you are supplied with a record showing what percentage of the cash return was interest and what percentage was principal.

The primary appeal of a Ginnie Mae is that the income is government-guaranteed, yet the yield will always be about a percentage point more than a Treasury bond with a ten-year maturity. Against that you must balance a number of disadvantages, minor and major.

Ginnie Maes are not quite as liquid as Treasury bonds—should you need to sell one, you'll lose a few percentage points of the security's value.

The income from a Ginnie Mae varies from month to month, depending on the pattern of home sales. Ginnie Maes are created from self-liquidating mortgages. **So, unlike a bond, you must discipline yourself to set aside a portion of each monthly payment or face the fact that you'll have nothing left at the end.**

These flaws are remediable—at a price. Mutual funds composed entirely of Ginnie Maes are now available for a minimum investment of $1,000. The mutual fund will buy back your shares at any time for their underlying asset value. Funds sold by brokers charge a "load," or fee, of up to 8 percent to buy shares. To avoid the fee, try one of these no-load funds marketed directly by an investment company:

> Dreyfus GNMA Fund
> (800) 645–6561—outside New York
> (718) 895–1206
>
> Lexington GNMA Income Fund
> (800) 526–0057
>
> Vanguard Fixed Income—GNMA Portfolio
> (800) 662–7447

Another alternative is to buy a Ginnie Mae unit trust from a big brokerage house like Merrill Lynch or Dean Witter. For a $1,000 minimum investment, you get a thin slice of a fixed pie composed of several million dollars' worth of Ginnie Maes. Brokers take an initial fee or "load" of 3 to 4 percent from your investment. But unlike the funds, there is little or no fee taken annually to reduce the net yield in following years.

Are Ginnie Maes right for you? Yes, if you are in a low tax bracket and want government-guaranteed income. The simplest way to invest is through one of the funds. **Otherwise buy older Ginnie Mae pass-through certificates that are selling below the face value of the underlying mortgages.** Homeowners with such bargain mortgages are far less likely to pay them off, so your income will last longer. When an owner does pay one off, you'll receive a cash windfall representing part of the difference between current price of the Ginnie Mae and the face value of the underlying mortgages.

Other Mortgage-Backed Securities

Ginnie Maes have proved so popular that a host of other mortgage-backed securities have come onto the market. The Federal Home Loan Mortgage Corporation, called Freddie Mac (cute, huh?), sells $25,000 "participation certificates" through brokers. Freddie Mac PCs are very similar to Ginnie Maes, but the payment of interest and principal is guaranteed by the corporation, not by the U.S. government.

Still, PCs are very safe. Freddie Mac maintains its own substantial reserves, and in any case, the underlying mortgages are government-guaranteed. The real drawback is that it can take as much as a year for Freddie Mac to make good on a defaulted mortgage. To make up for this flaw, PCs pay a little higher interest than Ginnie Maes.

Ready for more alphabet soup? Here's another for the pot. The Federal National Mortgage Association (Fannie Mae) issues a mortgage-backed security in $25,000 denominations, unimaginatively called the Mortgage Backed Security or MBS. MBSs are just like PCs, only Fannie Mae guarantees that you won't have to wait to collect on defaulted mortgage principal.

As noted before, Ginnie Maes (and Freddie Mac PCs and Fannie Mae MBSs) have a serious disadvantage. Since you don't know when homeowners are going to repay their individual mortgages, you don't know in advance how much money you'll be getting each month, how much interest you'll receive, or how long the investment will last. That is why the Collateralized Mortgage Obligation (CMO) was invented.

CMOs work like this: Freddie Mac, or a big investment banking house, issues a series of bondlike securities backed by a large pool of home mortgages. All the bondholders receive regular semiannual interest checks. But some of the bonds are designated "fast-pay," some "medium-pay," and some "slow-pay." "Fast-pay" CMOs receive all repayments of principal for the first few years, giving them a relatively short average life. When they are paid off, the next CMOs in line start to receive principal repayments. When they are paid off the third CMOs in line receive principal repayments, and so forth.

A CMO owner still doesn't know how to tell exactly how long the investment will last. But he or she does have a much better idea. The price of this greater certainty is a slightly lower yield. How much lower depends upon the quality of the underlying mortgages and the place in line: CMOs backed by government-guaranteed mortgages pay lower rates, as do CMOs designated as fast-pay. Most CMOs are sold by brokers. But they are increasingly available from banks, S&Ls, and even Sears stores in denominations as low as $1,000.

Sound complicated? It is a bit, but worth the trouble if you are determined to get the best deal for your money.

TIPS

$ High-yield, long-term securities can be good investments for conservative investors. But prudent investors should put no more than half their wealth in such inflation-vulnerable securities.

$ Treasury securities with maturities of ten years or more are easy to buy and sell, and free of risk of default. For most conservative investors that makes up for their one big disadvantage: somewhat lower interest.

$ Small investors wishing to own corporate bonds can reduce the risk and inconvenience by purchasing a bond mutual fund or unit trust instead.

$ GNMA (Ginnie Mae) "pass-through" certificates are government-guaranteed and pay higher interest than Treasury bonds. If you can't afford to plunk down the $25,000 minimum, buy $1,000 shares in a Ginnie Mae mutual fund.

$ Taxable, zero-coupon securities let you lock in high interest rates for tax-sheltered retirement accounts. Tax-exempt zeros provide no current income, but can be a good way to build a nest egg for the future. You must check carefully, though, to make sure they have no hidden "call" provision.

5

FREEDOM FROM THE TAX COLLECTOR

NOT LONG ago, investing was as much about reducing taxes as earning income. No more.

Look at the numbers. In 1981, the maximum tax rate was 70 percent; next year, it will be just 33 percent. What's more very few people will pay anything like the maximum rate: the average family of four living on $40,000 a year will owe less than $4,000 of it to Uncle Sam.

If taxes are less burdensome, they are also becoming more difficult to avoid. The legendary tax shelters—real estate, animal breeding, oil and gas drilling, equipment leasing—are dead. Ditto for capital gains preferences. And deductions that made retirement accounts the most popular of all shelters have been sharply curtailed.

Does that mean investors should stop worrying and learn to love the Internal Revenue Service? Not quite. First, there is the question of transition to the new tax system. In 1987, with tax reform only partially in effect, those with taxable incomes exceeding $45,000 will be in the 35 percent bracket. Even after 1987, many middle-income families living in high-tax states will discover they are still better off with "tax advantaged" investments. And virtually anyone lucky enough to earn $70,000 or more a year is likely to find that tax-planned investments make sense.

Tax-Exempt Bonds—What They Are

Tax-exempt bonds, casually referred to as "municipal" bonds because some are issued by municipalities, are the debts of tax-exempt entities. A decade ago, most tax-exempts were "general obligation" bonds backed by the taxing power of a state or local government or a school district. A minority were "revenue" bonds, backed by the revenues of a public authority like a turnpike or irrigation district. Since then, however, Congress has allowed tax-exempt revenue bonds to be used to build everything from fast-food restaurants in industrial development areas to private homes to industrial pollution control facilities.

Should you care which sort you buy? What counts most from the investor's view is yield and certainty of payment, which are only indirectly related to the issuer of the bond. However, under the new tax reform law, income from municipal bonds that serve a "private purpose" and were issued after August 1986 may not be fully tax-exempt. Earnings from these bonds count in the calculation of the new 21 percent alternate minimum tax.

Happily, this is not a concern for the vast majority of investors. Those who earn most of their income from investments and make heavy use of deductions for depreciation and medical expenses should be wary, though. If in doubt, check with your tax accountant.

Tax-exempt bonds are usually issued in "serial" form. A school district, for example, might sell $10 million worth of bonds to build a new building, with $500,000 worth coming due each year. This allows the taxing authority to pay off the debt slowly. And it permits investors to choose any maturity that suits. Bonds maturing in a year or more usually come in $5,000 denominations; shorter-term ones, typically bought only by banks and funds, come in $100,000 or even $1,000,000 chunks. By convention, however, the price of any size bond is quoted as a fraction of 100. For example, a bond selling for 85 percent of the price on the date of issue would be quoted at 85. A bond selling for 110 percent of the issue value would be quoted at 110.

Tax-exempts are sold through full-service brokerage firms like Dean Witter, A. G. Edwards, E. F. Hutton, Merrill Lynch, Paine Webber, Prudential/Bache, and Shearson/American Express, to name a few of the biggies. Each has offices in virtually every large and medium-sized city. Alternatively, you can buy tax-exempts from specialized bond dealers. However, since there is relatively little regulation over the way bonds are retailed to the public, neophytes would be wise to stick with a big full-service broker or one of the well-known specialized dealers like Lebenthal (800) 221–5822 or Ramirez (800) 221–4086. **Municipal bonds are usually sold in large lots. And, in truth, none of these firms will be particularly eager for your business unless you have $25,000 to invest.**

Tax-exempts with terms longer than a year pay interest every six months. Should you buy, say, one month before an interest payment date, you get the full payment. But the interest accrued over the previous five months will be added to the price you are charged for the bond. Until 1985 most tax-exempts were issued in anonymous "coupon" form. You, or a bank or broker working for you, literally clipped a coupon from the bond document and presented it for payment. But because of change in federal law, newly issued tax-exempts are "registered," much the way stock certificates are. **Interest payments are automatically mailed to you or transferred to your brokerage account.** That may be a bummer if you made the money to buy the bond by some illegal means and therefore don't want a paper trail linking the money to you. But for the rest of us, registration is a convenience.

Most tax-exempt bonds, like most taxable bonds, contain a "call" provision. This allows the issuer to buy back the bond after a specified number of years at a specified price, usually a bit above the initial selling price. Calls work entirely in favor of the borrower. If interest rates go up after the bond is issued, the value of the bond goes down and the issuer ignores the call provision. However, if interest rates fall, the value of the bond rises and the issuer gets to buy it back for a bargain price. **The bottom line: avoid bonds with call provisions, or at least figure the potential implications before you buy.**

Tax-Exempt Bonds—What to Look For

Safety. A primary concern is the likelihood the interest will be paid promptly, and the principal returned when the bond matures. You could try to check the creditworthiness of the bond issuer yourself. A far easier way, though, is to accept the opinion of one of the private credit rating agencies: Moody's or Standard and Poor's. For a fee paid by the bond issuer, they assign one of the following ratings:

	Moody's	**Standard and Poor's**
Best Quality	Aaa	AAA
Excellent Quality	Aa	AA

High Quality	A	A
Medium	Baa	BBB
Speculative	Ba	BB
Low Quality	B	B
Poor	Caa	CCC
In or Near Default	Ca	CC
Lowest Grade	C	C

The High Quality category (A) is probably the lowest with which conservative investors should feel comfortable. The next category down (Baa/BBB) might be worth considering if there is considerable difference in return and the investment is a small part of your assets. Remember, though, that there are serious limits on the reliability of bond ratings. The credit rating agencies are certainly conscientious. But all they can really measure is the amount of revenue behind a bond. There is simply no science to deciding whether, ten years from now, a city council will raise taxes because it is prudent to do so, or whether a judge will force a state to pay its bond interest before it pays its employees.

One way to minimize the risk of default is to buy only bonds that carry a federal government guarantee. Another is to buy bonds that have been insured by a private corporation. One such insurer is the American Municipal Bond Assurance Corporation (AMBAC), a subsidiary of the Baldwin-United Corporation. The other is the Municipal Bond Insurance Association (MBIA), a consortium of four giant insurance companies. Obviously neither AMBAC nor MBIA insurance is as good as a federal guarantee. But it would take a catastrophic series of defaults to deny the security of their coverage. Typically, MBIA-insured bonds are given a triple-A rating by the credit services.

Yield. Tax-exempt bonds pay lower interest than comparably secure taxable bonds. Thus tax-exempts should never be purchased for tax-deferred retirement accounts or by people in very low tax brackets. **In recent years, however, the difference in yield between taxable and tax-exempt bonds has narrowed so much that many people in the 28 percent tax bracket would benefit from owning them.** The tables on pages 44–46 should give you an idea of where you stand in 1987 and 1988. The tables underestimate the total benefits from tax exemption because they do not include state and local income taxes.

Note, too, that while the federal government does not tax municipal bonds, many state and local governments do, if the income is earned out of state. There are two ways around this dilemma. One is to stick with bonds issued in your own state. The other is to buy tax-exempts issued in Puerto Rico. The states treat Puerto Rico as if it were a part of the federal government. And states do not tax interest paid by the feds.

Liquidity. A corporate bond issued by AT&T can be sold in five minutes (and a very low commission paid on the sale) because AT&T bonds are known quantities. Not so the obligations of the Wawatosa-Mandarin-Goshen Consolidated School District. No one, it is safe to say, has heard of the W-M-G Consolidated School District, because I made it up. But relatively few of the thousands of agencies issuing tax-exempts carry much more credibility in the capital markets. It may take days to find a dealer who will take a small quantity of an obscure tax-exempt issue off your hands. And the spread between what the dealer will pay and what he or she expects to sell it for may be as much as 10 percent.

How to minimize such liquidity problems? **Stick with well-known heavily traded, high-quality issues, such as the general obligations of large state governments.** Or buy bonds with AMBAC or MBIA insurance. Far better yet, buy a tax-exempt unit trust (see page 47) from a sponsoring dealer who promises to make a market for the securities as long as they exist.

Special features. In recent years many issuers of taxable bonds have added features to their bonds in order to reduce risk or raise liquidity. Private insurance is one such feature. Yet newer ones include:

FLOATING RATE BONDS—The interest on these bonds is not fixed, but is adjusted every few weeks or months to track the yield on newly issued bonds. "Floaters" won't go down in value (or will go down less) when interest rates in the economy go up. On the other hand, the value won't go up when interest rates fall.

Single Return—1987

| | | To equal these tax-exempt returns: | | | | | |
		5%	6%	7%	8%	9%	10%
If your taxable income is:	Your tax bracket is:	You would have to earn this percentage on a taxable investment:					
16,800–27,000	28	6.94	8.33	9.72	11.11	12.50	13.89
27,000–54,000	35	7.69	9.23	10.77	12.31	13.85	15.38
54,000 +	38.5	8.13	9.76	11.38	13.01	14.63	16.26

OPTION TENDER BONDS—Sometimes called "put" bonds, these reverse the call privilege. You can sell the bond back to the issuer at a price fixed in advance. Again, the idea is that such a bond can't lose much of its value when interest rates rise.

PREREFUNDED BONDS—Some tax-exempt issuers wholly or partially back their bonds with U. S. Treasury bonds. Don't ask why; it's not worth the trouble to understand. What may be worth the trouble is to find such bonds because their yields may be higher than other, comparably secure bonds.

ZERO-COUPON BONDS—Zero-coupon tax-exempts do not pay interest directly. Instead they are issued at enormous discounts—thirty cents on the dollar for a bond due to mature in ten years, for example—and gradually gain market value until they are redeemed at full worth by the issuer. Zeros can truly lock in the investment by eliminating all uncertainty about what yield you'll be able to get, should you wish to reinvest the interest payments. Consider two possible catches, though, before buying one. First, some do contain call provisions, so the issuer can in fact buy them back for less than their full value before maturation. Second, they provide no current income, which could be a big drawback if you need the cash to pay the rent.

Joint Return—1987

If your taxable income is:	Your tax bracket is:	To equal these tax-exempt returns:					
		5%	6%	7%	8%	9%	10%
		You would have to earn this percentage on a taxable investment:					
28,000–45,000	28	6.94	8.33	9.72	11.11	12.50	13.89
45,000–90,000	35	7.69	9.23	10.77	12.31	13.85	15.38
90,000+	38.5	8.13	9.76	11.38	13.01	14.63	16.26

Single Return—1988

		To equal these tax-exempt returns:					
		5%	6%	7%	8%	9%	10%
If your taxable income is:	Your tax bracket is:	You would have to earn this percentage on a taxable investment:					
17,850–43,140	28	6.94	8.33	9.72	11.11	12.50	13.89
43,140–100,480	33	7.46	8.96	10.45	11.94	13.43	14.93
100,480 +	28	6.94	8.33	9.72	11.11	12.50	13.89

Joint Return—1988

		To equal these tax-exempt returns:					
		5%	6%	7%	8%	9%	10%
If your taxable income is:	Your tax bracket is:	You would have to earn this percentage on a taxable investment:					
29,750–71,900	28	6.94	8.33	9.72	11.11	12.50	13.89
71,900–171,090	33	7.46	8.96	10.45	11.94	13.43	14.93
171,090 +	28	6.94	8.33	9.72	11.11	12.50	13.89

Strategies

The high after-tax yield on municipal bonds is a powerful attraction to investors in the top tax brackets, particularly those living in high tax states. The poor liquidity is a powerful repellent. For relatively few readers—those with $50,000 they can comfortably lock up for a decade—it may well be worth the trouble to search out the right issue. Searching, incidentally, pays off because the poor liquidity of munis means there are occasionally very good buys to be had from people in a hurry to unload their investments. Luckily there are ways to get almost all the advantages of buying tax-exempts directly without having to deal with the disadvantages.

Tax-exempt unit trusts. This is one of the neatest inventions since the bacon cheeseburger. An investment company—a big broker or bond specialist—buys $30–$40 million worth of tax-exempt bonds, spreading the cash among a dozen or more different issues. The whole batch is divided into thousands of slices, each slice representing a tiny fraction of each issue owned by the trust. The investment company then resells these little units to the public, taking a 2–5 percent profit for its trouble.

It's clear enough what's in the deal for the investment company. What about the individuals who buy the units? For as little as $1,000, they get tax-exempt income from a diversified portfolio of bonds. Should one of the issuers default—an extremely unlikely occurrence since most unit trusts are created from bonds rated A or better—the investor loses only a few percentage points of his or her money. There are no coupons to clip. For a small fee taken from the income, the investment company mails out checks each month containing interest plus any principal from bonds that have been called by the issuer. **And should the need arise, it is easy to sell the units because the investment company sponsor guarantees to buy them back at the market value of the underlying bonds.**

Actually, the deal can get even better. Unit trusts have become so popular that it is now possible to tailor them to specialized needs. Some unit trusts contain bonds from single states (California, Massachusetts, Michigan, Minnesota, New York, Pennsylvania, Virginia), allowing investors to avoid state and local, as well as federal, taxes.

Others include insurance from AMBAC. Still others give you the option of automatic reinvestment of the interest payments at prevailing rates. A few contain floating-rate bonds, reducing the risk of capital losses should interest rates rise. Most contain bonds with very long maturities (twenty to thirty years). But a few have considerably shorter maturities, limiting the risks from an increase in interest rates.

The very latest idea is to mix regular high-yield bonds with deeply discounted, zero-coupon bonds. The interest paid out each month is lower. But the appreciation of the zero-coupon bonds in the batch means that you get more principal out in the end than you originally put in.

Unit trusts are available from any broker or bond dealer who sells municipal bonds. Note, though, that many brokers prefer to sell unit trusts packaged by their own firms. It pays to shop around, especially if you want a specialized feature like insurance against default.

Tax-exempt bond funds. In a tax-exempt unit trust the underlying investment is fixed. In a tax-exempt bond fund, the sponsoring company buys and sells securities in order to minimize risk and maximize yield. Why choose one rather than the other? In theory, the managers of the fund earn their way by keeping track of changing market conditions. In practice, bond funds sometimes do better than fixed portfolios, and sometimes they do worse. The big differences between the two are (a) the cost of getting in and out and (b) the current yield.

Sponsors of unit trusts take most of their profit up front, when you buy. So if you buy a unit this week and sell it next week, you are almost certain to lose between 2 and 5 percent of the investment. Many (not all) bond funds charge nothing to get in or out. But they take a much bigger chunk of the annual income, usually half a percentage point. Hence the choice depends on how long you expect to stay in. **If it's less than five years, stick with a fund. If it's more, you'll probably be better off with a unit trust.**

The following is a small selection of tax-exempt bond funds that do not charge a fee for purchase or sale:

Dreyfus Tax-Exempt Bond Fund
   (800) 645–6561—outside New York
   (800) 795–1206—in New York

Federated Tax-Free Income Fund
   (800) 245–4770

Safeco Municipal Bond Fund
   (800) 426–6730—outside Washington State
   (800) 562–6810—in Washington State

Scudder Managed Municipal Bond Fund
   (800) 225–2470

SteinRoe Managed Muni Fund
   (800) 621–0320—outside Illinois
   (312) 368–7826

Vanguard Group Municipal Bond Funds
   (800) 662–7447

These tax-exempt funds invest in lower-rated, somewhat riskier bonds, and thus can be expected to pay a percentage point or two more in current interest:

Fidelity High Yield Municipal Bonds
   (800) 544–6666—outside Massachusetts
   (617) 523–1919

Financial Tax-Free Income Shares
(800) 525–8085—outside Colorado
(800)525–9769—in Colorado

GIT Tax Free—High Yield
(800) 336–3063—outside Virginia
(800) 572–2050—in Virginia

Vanguard Municipal Bonds—High Yield
(800) 662–7447

These funds are exempt from state and local, as well as federal, taxes in their name state:

Dreyfus California Tax-Exempt Bond Fund
(800) 645–6561—outside New York
(718) 895–1206

Fidelity Massachusetts Tax-Free Portfolio
(800) 225–6190—outside Massachusetts
(617) 523–1919

Dreyfus New York Tax-Exempt Bond Fund
(800) 645–6561—outside New York
(718) 895–1206

Fidelity New York Tax-Free Portfolio
(800) 225–6190—outside Massachusetts
(617) 523–1919

Franklin New York Tax-Free Income Fund
(800) 632–2180

New York Muni Fund
(800) 528–6050—outside New York
(212) 747–9215

T. Rowe Price New York Tax-Free Bond Fund
(800) 638–5660

last alternative to consider. As noted before, it's risky to purchase even the safest long-term bond or shares in a fund that owns long-term bonds. If interest rates rise, you'll lose some of your principal. One way around the problem is to buy floating-rate bonds or option-tender bonds, discussed above. Both sorts of security prevent serious loss, should interest rates rise. But both also have serious shortcomings for small investors: poor liquidity; little room to diversify; relatively low yields.

One new mutual fund, the Principal Preservation Tax-Exempt Fund, offers a unique solution. It buys long-term bonds in order to get high yields. But at the same time, it hedges against a rise in interest rates much the way the treasurers of large corporations do, buying and selling a variety of fancy financial instruments such as option contracts on government securities.

Now for the bad news. The Principal Preservation Fund charges a load of about 5 percent. Still, investors might investigate it as a reasonable alternative to unit trusts, which also charge a load, or option-tender bonds, which are not liquid. Brokers are selling the fund in minimum units of $5,000. If you have difficulty getting a prospectus, call the fund's investment advisor, B. C. Ziegler and Company (800) 826–4600.

Tax Deferral

Why choose an investment that only defers taxation, when you could own a municipal bond (or fund or unit trust) that eliminates taxes entirely? Because even investors in the highest tax brackets must consider other characteristics of investments—namely risk, liquidity, and yield. One of the following conservative investments may better fit your needs.

Single premium deferred annuities. The name is a mouthful, but the product is pretty straightforward. A deferred annuity is a savings account maintained by a life insurance company. You deposit an initial sum of at least $5,000. The insurance company adds interest to the account at a guaranteed rate. The length of that guarantee, incidentally, varies from one to five years depending on the company. And the rate itself is usually about one percentage point less than you could earn by purchasing a taxable corporate bond.

Now for the tax gimmick. As long as the interest is left in the account untouched, you owe no taxes. This deferral allows you to earn interest on the full *pretax* value of the interest you have already accumulated. So even if you took the money out ten years later and paid all the taxes owed you'd be way ahead. Should you wish, the insurance company will trade your nest egg for a guaranteed monthly income on your retirement—that's why it is called a deferred annuity and why insurance companies got into the business in the first place.

Deferred annuities were once considered one of the safest of all nongovernment-guaranteed investments. The principal is secured by the assets of a life insurance company, which is subject to strict state regulation. And, unlike fixed-income investments such as bonds, the value of the account does not fluctuate as interest rates rise and fall.

This reputation for safety has been somewhat clouded by the financial troubles of the Baldwin-United, parent corporation of two big sellers of deferred annuities, National Investors Life Insurance Company and University Life Insurance.

The trustees of the bankrupt parent company and a number of brokerage houses that sold Baldwin-United annuities are dickering with state insurance officials over how much annuity holders will get back. Owners of deferred annuities issued by another troubled insurance company, Charter Security Life, will almost certainly end up with exactly what they paid for. Indeed, Charter may emerge as a strong, healthy insurer. But, in general, investors should be as prudent in buying deferred annuities as they are with other, reasonably secure but nonfederally guaranteed security.

How can you tell whether any specific insurance company is financially sound? **One shorthand method is to ask whether the company is licensed to do business in New York or California. These two states have especially tight regulatory standards.**

One more paragraph of caution. A deferred annuity is a very attractive investment for people who plan to maintain the account for long periods, preferably until retirement. But it can be a bad deal for those who expect to withdraw the money within a few years. Most companies charge a penalty of 7 percent for withdrawal in the first year, 6 percent in the second, 5 percent in the third, and so forth. To add insult to injury, the feds add 10 percent tax (along with any income tax owed) if the owner withdrawing the money is under age 59½.

Single premium deferred annuities are marketed by stockbrokers and insurance companies. **It is wise to shop around because the terms of the annuity—the interest rate, the guarantee period, the penalty for early withdrawal—vary from company to company.**

So far, we've been talking about deferred annuities, in which the insurance company guarantees a specific rate of interest for a few months at a time. How the company actually invests the money has nothing to do with your return. Another form of deferred annuity, called a variable annuity, gives the individual investor a chance for greater gain—or loss.

A variable annuity is, in essence, a mutual fund with tax advantages. You plunk down cash—typically a minimum of $5,000—which goes into a fund that buys stocks or bonds or money market securities. Earnings, less contractual fees, are plowed back into your kitty. When, and if you wish, the cash value of the account can be converted into an annuity paying a fixed monthly sum for life.

The big advantage to a deferred variable annuity over an ordinary mutual fund is that the earnings are sheltered from taxation until withdrawn. The disadvantage is that the sales charges and fees collected by the insurance company sponsor are often quite high, as are the penalties for withdrawal before retirement.

Is a variable annuity right for you? Only if you can afford to set aside the money for a considerable period, and then only if you can afford to bear the risk. Compare the specific policy with the universal life insurance alternative (see below). Be sure, too, to make maximum use of your IRA, Keogh, and/or salary reduction plan (see Chapter 7) before putting a penny in a variable annuity. The tax advantages are greater and the sales charges are usually smaller.

As with fixed-return deferred annuities, it's very important to shop around among insurance agents and brokers. Any seller who is reluctant to spell out the fees in detail and provide information on the fund's track record is to be avoided.

Two variable annuities worth a close look:

> Phoenix VA Stock Fund
> Phoenix Mutual Life
>
> Guardian Stock Fund/ValuGuard II
> Guardian Life.

Both are fairly aggressive stock funds which managed to outperform the market averages between 1984 and 1986. These and other variable annuities are now tracked in the Market Week statistical tables at the back of *Barron's Financial Weekly*.

Universal life insurance. Life insurance is insurance, not an investment. But most life insurance is sold in the form of "whole life" policies, which is really a combination of life insurance and a savings plan. You pay in more than the actual cost of insuring your life, allowing you to accumulate a nut of tax-deferred savings, which is returned to you with interest when you cancel the policy or retire.

Trouble is, very few whole life policies pay a decent rate of interest on the accumulating cash, and most won't even tell you what rate they pay. Moreover, if you cancel within the first few years, huge charges are usually subtracted from the savings before it is returned.

For obvious reasons, sophisticated insurance buyers have increasingly switched to "term" insurance, which is pure, no-frills life insurance that accumulates no savings. To lure these defectors back to the more profitable part of the business, insurers created a new product called "universal" life.

Universal life is really an amalgam of term insurance and a souped-up deferred annuity. You pay premiums, part of which covers the cost of the insurance. The rest goes into an account that accumulates interest at a high rate—roughly the rate on corporate bonds. Uncle Sam collects no taxes while the money is in the account. Best of all, withdrawals are not taxed as income unless they exceed the total premium paid each year.

Who is a candidate for universal life? People in high tax brackets who would otherwise buy term insurance and invest their savings in highly liquid securities. Remember, however, that life insurance is a jungle; no two policies are exactly alike. Most universal life policies charge a large flat initiation fee, so if you cancel the policy within a year or two you end up way behind. Some nail you even more, charging a fee for withdrawals made in the first few years. So you must shop around to find a good deal. Statistics on the share value of specific universal life policies can be found in the Market Week section of *Barron's Financial Weekly*.

A group called the National Insurance Consumer Organization has evaluated the universal life policies on the market and says the best buy is sold by USAA Life. Write USAA Building, San Antonio, TX 78288; or phone (800) 531–8000. To cut costs, USAA policies are sold directly by mail rather than through insurance agents.

TIPS

$ Many individual investors with incomes exceeding $30,000 (and many families with incomes exceeding $50,000) can earn more from tax-exempt securities than taxable ones.

$ For all but the richest and most-sophisticated investors, buying shares in a tax-exempt bond unit trust or tax-exempt bond fund makes more sense than buying the bonds directly.

$ Deferred annuities and universal life insurance can be attractive ways for high-tax-bracket families to earn high, safe yields. But you must shop carefully to get good buys. And to enjoy the full advantages they can provide, you must be prepared to let the money accumulate for many years.

6

BULLISH
ON AMERICA

TAKING A FLYER in the stock market was once a great American pastime. And no wonder. If your parents had invested $10,000 in a randomly chosen, diverse basket of common stocks in 1926, then hung on for fifty years reinvesting all dividends, they would have amassed a $900,000 fortune! Or try a less ambitious savings scenario. Suppose you (or your parents) had set aside $10,000 in 1947 and let your luck run in the stock market for twenty years. You would have ended up with a not inconsiderable $153,000.

Why, then, does nearly everyone these days have a slightly bruised feeling about the stock market? Consider what would have happened if you'd left that $153,000 in the market past 1967. Adjusting for inflation, the value of your stocks would have dropped to $90,000 by 1974. Things picked up thereafter. Again adjusting for inflation, the $90,000 would have become $125,000 by 1981. Even so, you would have been a whole lot better off buying a house (or farmland, or Treasury bills, or gold . . . you name it).

Great fortunes have been made in stocks in the last few years, and no doubt great fortunes will be made in the next few. But history should make us all humble. **Don't put more in stocks—especially volatile stocks—than you can afford to lose.**

Buying Stocks—Some Basics

Common stock is fractional ownership in a corporation. Buy one share of General Motors, and you own 0.0000032 percent of the company. Like the owner of any business, what's left after the creditors, the employees, the suppliers, and the Internal Revenue Service have been satisfied is yours. Most companies pay out a fraction of after-tax profits as cash dividends every three months, retaining the rest to invest in the business.

How much is a share of GM stock worth? The share is a claim on the future profits of the company. If you knew with any certainty what GM's future profits would be (and what return alternative investments would pay), any business school grad could give you the formula for calculating the "present value" of your claim.

But no one really knows how well cars will sell in 1989, what they will cost to make, and so forth. So the market price of a stock is really a guess about what the last buyer and seller thought about the company's prospects. Or, if you insist on looking at the wheels within the wheels, it is what the last buyer thought other people would be willing to pay for the stock next week or next year.

The market's view of a stock can be summarized in two shorthand readings. A stock's price/earnings ratio, the market price of the stock divided by the current annual after-tax profit, says something about the market's optimism. **The higher this "PE" ratio, the more people are willing to bet that the company will be profitable in the future.** Of course, companies that are not currently making a profit can hardly be judged this way.

The second measure is the current dividend divided by the share price, or the "yield." This number looks a lot like an interest rate. And for stocks (such as electric utilities) that are traditionally purchased by investors seeking high, secure current income, that is not a bad way to read the yield. But dividends are generally taxed as ordinary income to the recipient. So many successful companies have an incentive to pay little or no dividend, plowing all the cash back into new plants and equipment.

Brokers buy and sell stocks through nine different domestic exchanges (and many foreign ones), the most important being the New York and American exchanges. But many stocks, including those of some large successful corporations, are exchanged "over the counter" in a computerized system that links brokers together. **From your perspective, it hardly matters where or how the transaction takes place, since most trades,**

on or off a major stock exchange, are now done by computer according to strict rules.

Daily newspaper listings from the New York and American exchanges typically look like this:

52-Week High	Low	Stock	Div	Yld %	PE Ratio	Sales 100s	High	Low	Last	Chg.
75¼	39	GMot	2.40	3.4	15	7179	71⅜	70	70	−1

Over the last fifty-two weeks, the highest price General Motors stock sold for was $75.25; the lowest was $39.00. The dividend per share paid over the last twelve months was $2.40. The yield (remember, that's the last twelve months' dividend divided by current price) is 3.4 percent. The current price of the stock is fifteen times GM's earnings over the past twelve months. A total of 717,900 shares changed hands on this day (making GM one of the twenty or thirty most actively traded stocks on the New York Exchange). During the day's trading, some investors paid as much as $71.37 a share, some as little as $70.00. The last trade of the day was at $70.00, down a dollar from the last trade the previous day.

The prices listed are actually a little more than you would receive as a seller (and a little less than you would pay as a buyer), because brokers take commissions from buyers and sellers. There are no longer any government rules setting commission rates, and they vary widely. **In general, though, the higher the dollar value of the transaction, the smaller the percentage to the broker.** More about broker commissions later.

Stock Market Advice

The way to make a lot of money is to buy a stock when it is cheap and sell it when it is expensive. For this you paid $3.95? Be grateful—most stock market advice costs a lot more and is just about as useful. Advisers and advice can be classified in three forms.

Tipsters say they know something about a company the rest of the world has yet to discover: that it is about to be granted a valuable patent, that it is about to be bought by another company, that it is about to announce lower-than-expected earnings for the last quarter, and so on. Trouble is, genuine inside information is rarely available. When it is, no one is going to sell it to you for peanuts. Tipsters depend on the selective quality of memory to hold on to their clients: everyone likes to remember the winners and everyone likes to forget the losers.

Chartists believe that stock prices follow statistical patterns partially or wholly unrelated to earnings prospects. They base their advice on tortuous mathematical analyses of the volume of stock sales, recent price movements of the stock, other stocks in the industry, and so forth. Chartists have achieved a certain respectability over the years, enough so that all large brokerage firms with research departments employ them. Sometimes a chartist will have a hot streak, predicting market trends very successfully. But sometimes gamblers have hot streaks in Las Vegas, predicting how many little black dots will appear faceup when the dice are rolled. **There is little evidence chartists are doing anything real.**

Fundamentalists (no, this has nothing to do with the Bible) are business school types at heart. They work hard both to estimate the future earnings of companies and to identify stocks that seem to have unjustifiably low price/earnings ratios by comparison with other companies in their industries. Many economists, who might otherwise be sympathetic with the way fundamentalists do their jobs, say the exercise is futile. Stock markets, they say, react rapidly and rationally to the available information. So by the time you get the news, it is already too late to buy or sell.

The economists may be right—most of the time. It is usually very hard to test the quality of the fundamentalist advice offered by brokers' research departments because suggestions to buy and sell are unsystematically offered. But a lot of people claim to have profited fairly consistently by sticking with fundamentals. **And one source of fundamentalist advice, the Value Line Investment Survey, has shown that its followers do make more money when the stock market goes up and lose less when the market goes down.**

Buying Stocks on Your Own

Should you buy and sell on your own? Millions of Americans do, often as not, as a hobby. But if the goal is to make money in a prudent, calculated fashion, consider the problems first.

Even the most sensible stock market strategies depend on estimates of probabilities. So it is important to avoid putting your nest egg in one basket. **Buy at least half a dozen stocks from different industries.** To diversify this way on your own requires a fairly large commitment of cash.

If you invest less than, say, $2,000 in a stock, or buy less than a hundred shares of any stock (a so-called odd lot), you will pay steep commissions. So to buy half a dozen stocks requires a minimum commitment of $12,000.

Still interested? Most small investors choose stocks on the advice of friends and brokers. **Most small investors also do poorly in the stock market, profiting less than the market average in booms, losing more in slumps.** In fact, some Wall Street cynics track statistics on which stocks are being bought and which sold in very small quantities (presumably by small investors), and then do the opposite.

The advice from brokers has three drawbacks.

(a) *It is expensive*. There is rarely a charge for research reports or specific advice. But so-called full-service brokers must be compensated somehow for the time they spend providing it. "Somehow" turns out to be in high commissions.

(b) *It is shopworn.* Big brokerage houses have hundreds of thousands of customers, all of whom have access to the same research. If you are the 4,000th person to hear that Alpha Synergistics has a hot new computer memory that is the envy of Silicon Valley, the information isn't worth much.

(c) *It is unobjective*. Brokers make money when you buy or sell. They make no money when you hang on to what you have. The vast majority of brokers are honest people who wish their clients well. But they have a natural preference for "action" that can make investing more exciting than profitable.

Is there a practical alternative? **Buy fundamentalist advice from the Value Line Investment Survey, then follow it slavishly with a minimum of six stocks, buying and selling through the least-expensive "discount" broker you can find.** That won't necessarily make you a lot of money. But it is the cheapest way to plug in to the same sort of fundamentalist system used by the best professional money managers.

The Value Line Investment Survey costs a whopping $425 a year. But you can get a ten-week trial subscription for a somewhat less nasty $55. The first issue, incidentally, includes a smart, readable explanation about how fundamentalists analyze the market.

Value Line Investment Survey
711 Third Avenue
New York, NY 10017
   (800) 633–2252, Ext. 281

Discount brokers usually don't give you advice. Nor do they congratulate you when you make money, console you when you lose money, or send you a card at Christmas. The clerk who answers the phone won't even know you have an account until you provide the number. **But discount brokers *do* process buy-and-sell orders, hold your securities for government-insured safekeeping, and provide records for taxes.**

Finding a discount broker is easy; they advertise all over the place. Finding the cheapest one is hard, because their prices change frequently, some charge for record-keeping and some don't, and the cost often varies with the number of orders you place each year.

How, then, to choose? Mark Coler, an astute analyst of the discount broker scene, distinguishes between "share brokers" and "value brokers." Share brokers weigh their charges by the number of shares bought or sold. So if you're buying relatively few shares—say 100 shares of a $50 stock— they're generally cheaper. Value brokers' fees are more closely linked to the dollar value of your transaction. So if you are buying a lot of shares— say 1,000 shares of a $5 stock—they're generally cheaper.

What should investors do who have little idea in advance whether they will be buying cheap stocks in large lots or expensive stocks in small lots? If you plan to trade a lot (hardly a recommended practice for those with modest sums to invest) set up two accounts, one at a share broker and one at a value broker. The compromise is to choose a discount broker with a mixed "share/value" price formula.

The very abbreviated list below is divided along Coler's lines. Keep in mind, though, that service counts as well as price. A discount broker who consistently provides good service, such as immediate confirmations by telephone and efficient record-keeping, may be worth paying a little extra for.

One last point. Hundreds of banks have begun offering brokerage services. It could pay to call a few local ones to compare rates and services.

Share Brokers:

Haas Securities
  (800) 621–1410—outside Illinois
  (800) 872–1139—in Illinois

Ovest Securities
  (800) 221–5713—outside New York
  (212) 425–3003

Pace Securities
(800) 221–1660—outside New York
(212) 490–6363

Pacific Brokerage Services
(800) 421–8395—outside California
(800) 421–3214—in California

StockCross
(800) 225–6196—outside Massachusetts
(800) 392–6104—in Massachusetts

Wall Street Discount
(800) 221–7990—outside New York
(212) 747–5013

Value Brokers

Marquette de Bary
(800) 221–3305—outside New York
(212) 425–5505

Fidelity/Source
(800) 225–2097—outside Massachusetts
(800) 882–1269—in Massachusetts

Charles Schwab
(800) 648–5300—outside California
(800) 792–0988—in California

Mixed Share/Value Brokers

Discount Brokerage
(800) 221–5088—outside New York
(212) 943–8500

Muriel Siebert
(800) 821–8200—outside New York
(212) 248–0600

Parker, Alexander
(800) 221–4872—outside New York
(212) 522–5629

Quick and Reilly
(800) 221–5220—outside New York
(212) 522–8712

Open-End Mutual Funds

A very practical alternative to buying common stocks is to buy shares in an "open-end" mutual fund. They work exactly like the bond funds described in other chapters. You send a minimum of $1,000 (sometimes less) to an investment company, which pools your money with others' to invest in stocks. With no-load funds there are no sales charges, so the entire amount is invested on your behalf. The investment company profits by charging an annual fee per share, sometimes related to the success of the fund. The fund uses its best judgment to buy and sell for maximum profit, passing all dividend income (after expenses) on to you. You may at any time sell back your shares to the fund for cash.

The potential advantages of a common stock mutual fund are the same as those of a bond fund: professional management, diversification, and convenience. A pro at the helm may or may not help. Funds that do spectacularly well when the market is going up are apt to do spectacularly badly when the market is going down. Still, there is hope. Diversification on the other hand is a clear blessing; as little as $1,000 allows you to own a piece of several hundred stocks. So, too, is the convenience of having someone else keep the records.

Once you've decided to buy into a no-load mutual fund, you still have to decide which mutual fund. For unlike bond funds, their objectives vary widely.

Income funds. These funds generate a lot of current income by investing heavily in high-dividend stocks such as electric utilities. Many also mix corporate bonds and preferred stocks (really a version of bond) with common stocks to create the highest-possible current yield. The value of such funds, like their underlying stocks, is that they are likely to be very sensitive to interest rates. **Consider them as an alternative to a long-term bond fund or other long-term fixed-income investments.**

AMA Income
(800) 523–0864—outside Pennsylvania
(215) 825–0400

61

Dreyfus Convertible Securities
    (800) 645–6561—outside New York
    (718) 895–1206

Fidelity Puritan
    (800) 544–6666—outside Massachusetts
    (617) 523–1919

Financial Industrial Income
    (800) 525–8085—outside Colorado
    (800) 525–9769—in Colorado

Nicholas Income
    (414) 272–6133

Northeast Investors Trust
    (800) 225–6704—outside Massachusetts
    (617) 523–3588

Vanguard Wellesley Fund
    (800) 662–7447

Balanced funds. These funds mix objectives of current income and capital appreciation. **They are a good bet for investors who want to participate in stock market booms without risking heavy losses when the market turns sour.**

Axe-Houghton Fund B
    (800) 431–1030—outside New York
    (914) 631–8131

Evergreen Total Return
    (800) 635–0003—outside New York
    (914) 698–5711

Gateway Option Income
    (800) 354–6339—outside Ohio
    (513) 248–2700

Loomis-Sayles Mutual
    (617) 578–4200

Safeco Income Fund
    (800) 426–6730—outside Washington State
    (800) 562–6810—in Washington State

Vanguard Wellington
(800) 662–7447

Growth funds. These funds push hard for capital appreciation. They sometimes pay small dividends, but **the idea is to play the market for maximum gain.** Not surprisingly, they are the most volatile; tread carefully. One other point: when growth funds do well, their managers sometimes get greedy. A number (none, to date, on this list) have recently switched from no-load to "small-load" funds, charging a few percentage points to buy or sell shares. Check the prospectus carefully before you buy.

Acorn Fund
(312) 621–0630

Boston Company Capital Appreciation
(800) 225–5267

Copley Tax Managed Fund
(617) 674–8459

Evergreen Fund
(800) 635–0003—outside New York
(914) 698–5711

Fairmont Fund
(502) 636–5633

GIT Equity Trust—Special Growth
(800) 336–3063—outside Virginia
(800) 572–2050—in Virginia

Neuberger and Berman Manhattan Fund/Partners Fund
(800) 367–0770—outside New York
(212) 850–8300

International funds. These funds invest in foreign stocks and securities. Since the assets they own are denominated in foreign currencies, they appreciate when the dollar falls. So they are useful as a hedge against depreciating U.S. currency. Watch it, though—if the dollar rises in value, these mutual funds will probably be losers.

G. T. Pacific Growth Fund
(800) 824–1580

T. Rowe Price International
(800) 638–5660—outside Maryland
(301) 547–2308

Scudder International
(800) 225–2470

Transatlantic Fund
(800) 233–9164—outside New York
(212) 747–0440

Index funds. Suppose you don't have any idea which stocks are winners (very smart), and you don't believe anybody else does, either (pretty smart). But you still want to diversify your assets by putting part of your money in the stock market. An index fund buys all important stocks and holds on to them, so that a share in the fund should closely track the ups and downs of the stock market. The only index fund available to small investors is:

Vanguard Index Trust
(800) 662–7447

Precious metals. Many people view gold, silver, platinum, palladium, and other metals as the ultimate hedge against inflation. These no-load funds largely invest in corporations that mine the metals; many of the stocks are South African:

Bull and Bear Golconda Fund
(800) 847–4200

Lexington Gold Fund
(800) 526–0057

United Services Gold Shares
(800) 824–4653

Closed-End Mutual Funds

Open-end mutual funds swell and shrink with investor interest, as individuals put money in and take money out. Closed-end mutual funds are like common stocks—you buy and sell shares from other owners through the stock exchanges, not from the fund itself. One obvious disadvantage is that no one promises to buy your shares at a moment's notice for their underlying value. Another is that you must pay regular brokerage commissions to trade shares.

Why, then, would anyone prefer a closed-end fund? For one thing, open-end funds are prisoners of market enthusiasm. Since they ebb and flow with the market, fund managers are under pressure to buy stock when everyone else is buying and to sell when everyone else is selling. **Closed-end funds have the freedom to buck trends, to look for bargains when stocks are out of favor.**

Then, too, closed-end funds sometimes sell for less than the underlying value of the securities they own; the figures are printed in most Sunday newspapers. This is slightly bizarre, since one might expect investors to pay extra to buy a well-managed fund. Whatever the reason, the discount effectively gives your dollars more investment punch.

As you can see from this abbreviated list, closed-end funds vary widely in objective.

Adams Express—conservative stocks, mostly high-yield blue chips.

ASA Limited—high-dividend South African stocks; mostly gold mines.

First Australia Fund—Australian securities.

France Fund—French securities.

Italy Fund—Italian securities.

Japan Fund—Japanese securities.

Korea Fund—Korean securities.

Lehmann Corporation—balanced, highly diversified portfolio.

Mexico Fund—Mexican securities.

Petroleum and Resources Corporation–energy and natural resources stocks.

Scandinavia Fund—Scandinavian stocks.

TIPS

$ The stock market is a place to win big or lose big. Invest only in what you understand and never more than a modest portion of your total savings.

$ Buying stocks on your own requires at least a $12,000 stake and preferably much more. Less prevents adequate diversification.

$ No-load mutual funds can give you most of the benefits of picking your own stocks, without the need for a deep pocket.

$ Stock tips are generally worthless. The only systems that work with any consistency are rooted in the "fundamentals."

$ If you are picking your own stocks, it probably makes sense to buy advice based on the fundamentals, then place your order through a discount broker.

$ An indexed mutual fund lets you bet on the stock market without betting on any single stock.

7

GILDING THE GOLDEN YEARS

THERE HAVE ALWAYS been good reasons to save for retirement, like being able to eat something better than Big Macs after the paychecks stop coming. Now there are two more.

Reason number one. After its brush with insolvency, Social Security is alive and resting comfortably. But the old days of big increases in benefits are surely over. Medical coverage has also been tightened, reducing that portion of retirees' hospital bills covered by government insurance. **It's become unrealistic for people planning their retirement to count on Social Security for much more than basic subsistence.**

Reason number two. What Uncle Sam taketh with the left hand, he restoreth with the right. The amount of money that can be sheltered in retirement accounts has been reduced by the 1986 tax reform law. Moreover, lower tax rates reduce the immediate tax savings. But the incentives for putting aside cash in an individual retirement account, Keogh plan, or salary reduction plan (401 (k) plan) are still quite substantial.

This chapter is devoted to explaining how to set up these three types of accounts, and offering advice on what to put in them. Don't forget, though, there are other tax-advantaged ways to save for retirement, specifically, tax-exempt bonds, deferred annuities, U. S. savings bonds, and universal life insurance. Read about each before deciding where to put your nest egg.

Individual Retirement Accounts

What they are. Known as an IRA, the individual retirement account is available to anyone who has employment income. Individuals may contribute up to 100 percent of the first $2,000 they earn each year. In other words, if you earned just $800 doing part-time work, you could contribute the entire $800. Earn $2,000 and contribute $2,000. But that's the limit: earn $20,000 and you still have a maximum contribution of $2,000.

Where two spouses are working, each can put away a maximum of $2,000; the funds must go into separate accounts. A contributor with a nonearning spouse may put away up to $2,250. In these so-called spousal accounts, specific portions of each contribution to the IRA must be set aside in each spouse's name.

Any contribution to an IRA for income earned in 1986 (such contributions must be made by April 15, 1987) is deductible from your 1986 taxable income, even if you don't itemize other deductions. The deductibility of contributions for 1987 depends on your income and on your eligibility for a pension from your employer. Those not covered by a pension plan are free to deduct, no matter how much they earn. However, workers who are covered face new limits.

Let's assume you are covered (if in doubt, check with your employer). If you are single and have an adjusted gross income of $25,000 or less, 1987 IRA contributions remain fully deductible. Ditto for married couples with a combined income of $50,000. Above those limits, the amount you can deduct is phased out at the rate of $200 for every extra $1,000 in income. Thus a single taxpayer with an income of $27,000 could deduct up to $1,600—$400 less than the old maximum. Similarly, a worker with taxable earnings of $34,000 could deduct just $200.

Interest, dividends, and other income earned on money in the IRA is not taxed until you withdraw it. But be careful. You pay a 10 percent penalty tax above and beyond income taxes owed on any withdrawals of deducted contributions or tax-deferred earnings before age 59. Note that withdrawals of deducted contributions are treated differently from withdrawals of nondeducted contributions. In order to keep the two sorts of contributions straight, it will almost certainly make sense to keep separate IRA accounts.

What is legally discouraged before age 59 is legally encouraged after age 70. You must begin drawing money from the IRA by that age. If you fail to do so, Uncle Sam slaps a tax on the money he thinks you should have withdrawn to support your retirement. The actual formula for calculating the minimum drawdown rate needed to avoid any penalty is quite complicated. But when the time comes, the corporate "custodian" of your IRA should be able to provide the details.

It is legal to borrow money to put into an IRA. And if that is the only way you can afford to do it at the moment, it may make sense. It is not legal, though, to use money or securities in an IRA as collateral for a loan.

You can contribute to an IRA anytime during the calendar year. Actually the law is more generous, allowing IRAs to be set up and contributions made until April 15 of the following year. Thus on April 15, 1988, you will still be able to make a 1987 contribution to your IRA and still deduct the contribution from your 1987 taxable income.

You can change "custodians" (the legal jargon for the institution that manages your IRA) as often as you like, simply by telling the custodian where to send the money and paying any penalty fees—watch it, they can be substantial—specified in your IRA agreement. You can set up as many different IRA accounts as you like, provided your contributions in total don't exceed the maximum permitted by law. It is also legal to "roll over" an IRA once a year, taking physical possession of the assets in your IRA. This could prove quite handy if you needed to use the money temporarily. But beware: if the cash (or other assets) isn't put into another IRA within sixty days, you must pay income tax . . . and the special 10 percent penalty tax, too.

Why they are terrific. An IRA gives you a convenient, reasonably flexible way to set aside cash for retirement. But that's only the beginning. IRAs offer an immediate tax break to most middle-income families. And since interest, dividend, and capital appreciation income earned within the account is not taxed until withdrawn, your savings accumulate faster.

Just how much this special tax treatment can benefit you is easy to show. Say you set aside $2,000 a year for thirty years in an IRA that, on average, earns 8 percent interest a year. After thirty years you will have accumulated $244,692.

Now consider a world without IRAs in which you set aside the same $2,000 of pretax income each year. Suppose you are in the 30 percent tax bracket including state and local taxes. After paying taxes on the $2,000 you'd have $1,400 to invest. Suppose you can earn the same 8 percent interest rate, only here it is fully taxable in the year it is earned. At the end of thirty years, you'd have $108,970.

Why they are not quite as terrific as advertised. Around tax time, when banks are promoting their IRA accounts, newspapers are full of charts showing just how rich you'd be on retirement if you only opened an account now.

Receive an Average Annual Return of:

Put $2,000 a year in an IRA for:	7%	8%	9%	10%	11%
			and You'll Retire with:		
10 years	$ 29,567	$ 31,291	$ 33,121	$ 35,062	$ 37,123
20 years	$ 87,730	$ 98,846	$111,529	$126,005	$142,530
30 years	$202,146	$244,692	$297,150	$361,887	$441,826

These calculations are accurate. Actually the figures are modest compared to some of the equally accurate calculations made a few years ago, when interest rates were running as high as 14 percent. Just imagine if you put aside $2,000 a year for thirty-five years at 14 percent interest; you'd have $1,581,346!

But think about it for a moment and you'll see the catch. The reason banks could offer 14 percent interest to depositors back in 1980 (or even 7 percent interest today) is because inflation makes it possible to lend out the money at high rates. If the inflation rate fell, so would the interest offered on IRAs. **So in order to make any sense of those enormous IRA retirement payouts far in the future, you have to adjust either the interest rate used in calculation, or the purchasing power of the dollars received on retirement.**

Economists have observed that over long periods of time interest rates average about 3 percent more than the rate of inflation. Plug a real (that is, after-inflation) interest rate of 3 percent into the same IRA calculations and you'd find:

$2,000 a year for ten years yields $23,616 (preinflation dollars).

$2,000 a year for twenty years yields $55,353 (preinflation dollars).

$2,000 a year for thirty years yields $98,005 (preinflation dollars).

What does all this mumbo-jumbo really boil down to? IRAs are indeed a fine way to save for retirement, especially if you start one fairly early in your working life so the money has a chance to accumulate. **Begin this year putting aside the maximum contribution, continue contributing for several decades, and you'll undoubtedly end up with a nice piece of change.** No one can say with certainty what portion of your retirement needs you will be able to cover with the proceeds. But in terms of today's purchasing power, the IRA nest egg you create is a lot more likely to be worth $98,000 than the $202,000, $361,000, or $441,000 shown in the table.

Where to start an IRA (and what investments to make with the money). The law gives you enormous flexibility in choosing the place to put your IRA. And, as already noted, it lets you move your IRA quite easily, should you change your mind. The decision should in part be based on how much risk you are willing to accept to increase the probable yield, in part on how much time and energy you want to put into managing the money.

Banks, savings and loans, credit unions. These are the safest places to maintain an IRA. Like any federally insured deposit, IRAs are covered against loss up to $100,000. Banks, S&Ls, and credit unions rarely charge a fee either to set up an IRA or to maintain one. A few do charge maintenance fees, though, and almost all charge a fee for transferring the account to another custodian. So read the fine print.

Virtually all banks promote special IRA certificates of deposit, paying whatever interest rate they care to offer. Some of these certificates have a yield that's fixed when you buy it; some have a variable yield that goes up and down over time along with general interest-rate levels. But there is no government regulation limiting the type of savings deposit that can be used with a bank IRA. Some banks, for example, allow you to keep the proceeds in money market accounts, six-month certificates, or even ten-year fixed-interest certificates of deposit.

The most conservative way to invest a bank IRA is to commit your funds for the shortest possible time. You lose a bit if interest rates happen to decline. But over long periods of time, the changing yield should keep you well ahead of inflation. This strategy also allows you to move the funds without interest penalty, should you later change your mind.

Don't assume that all banks offer the same terms. For the moment, savings and loan associations and savings banks seem a little hungrier for the IRA business than do commercial banks. They thus are likely to offer somewhat higher interest and more flexible investment options. But terms vary enormously, and the only way to find the best deal is to let your fingers do the walking.

Mutual funds. Almost all mutual funds—companies that pool the money from individuals to invest (see Chapter 6)—are happy to set up IRA accounts. And since mutual funds buy everything from stock in Japanese conglomerates to South African gold mine shares to electric utility bonds, the possibilities are virtually limitless. Common sense suggests, though, that IRAs don't belong in certain types of mutual funds. **It would be silly,** for example, to invest in a fund that is tax-exempt, since IRA accounts are fully shielded from taxation anyway.

More eligible are mutual funds with conservative goals—money market funds, or funds that invest in stocks and bonds with an eye toward maximum current income. That way there is far less chance that you'll retire with little to show for your savings effort.

Is an IRA with a mutual fund right for you? Consider first the disadvantages. All but the money market funds are vulnerable to market risks: your nest egg will change in value as the stock market fluctuates, and/or interest rates change. Then, too, mutual funds virtually always charge fees for maintaining the accounts. Some go much further, levying a heavy sales fee, or "load," each time you add money to the IRA.

What mutual funds can give you that banks can't is the potential for very substantial gain. **If you are prepared to take calculated risks with the IRA portion of your retirement assets, but are not eager to choose individual stocks yourself, a mutual fund may be right for you.** The smart way to set up a mutual-fund IRA is with an investment company that (a) runs a variety of funds and allows you to switch from one to the other at little or no cost and (b) runs funds that do not deduct a sales fee from your IRA contributions. Here is a short list of companies with good investment records that meet both criteria:

Dreyfus Funds
    (800) 645–6161—outside New York
    (718) 895–1206

Fidelity Funds
    (800) 225–6190—outside Massachusetts
    (617) 523–1918

Neuberger and Berman Funds
    (800) 367–0770—outside New York
    (212) 850–8300

Safeco Funds
    (800) 426–6730—outside Washington State
    (800) 562–6810—in Washington State

Scudder Funds
    (800) 225–2470—outside Massachusetts
    (617) 482–3990

SteinRoe Funds
    (800) 621–0615—outside Illinois
    (312) 368–7800

T. Rowe Price Funds
    (800) 638–5660—outside Maryland
    (301) 547–2308

USAA Funds
    (800) 531–8181—outside Texas
    (512) 690–6062

Value Line Funds
    (800) 223–0818—outside New York
    (800) 522–5217—in New York

Vanguard Funds
    (800) 662–7447

Insurance companies. Most life insurance companies vigorously promote annuities as IRAs. On first glance the idea is appealing. Your money purchases annuity contracts that, once you retire, guarantee a monthly check as long as you live. Trouble is, the insurance companies typically charge very heavy fees for starting an IRA annuity. If you ever wish to switch to a different custodian, they sock you again with heavy fees. And as if that weren't bad enough, the companies do not necessarily provide the most annuity income for the dollars they do leave in the account.

It just doesn't make sense, then, to set up an IRA with an insurance company. You always have the option of purchasing an annuity at retirement by rolling over the proceeds from a bank or mutual-fund IRA.

Your employer. Although it has yet to become common practice, companies may set up IRAs for the convenience of their employees. Employers may not contribute to these IRAs; nor are they permitted to specify how the money is to be invested. But they are allowed, at the election of the individual employee, to deduct IRA contributions from paychecks.

These so-called voluntary-contribution IRAs make some sense if you lack the discipline to save without a payroll deduction. Note, though, that by spreading your contributions across the year, rather than putting the money into the IRA early in the year, you lose some tax-free interest accumulation.

Brokerage houses. It is possible to manage the investments in your own IRA, with a stockbroker acting as the custodian. The advantage (or disadvantage?) is that you control the account. Remember, though, that in the early years of an IRA, the amount of money available to invest will be quite small, making it difficult (if not impossible) to spread your money among several different stocks-and-bonds investments without incurring very high broker charges relative to the size of your nest egg (if you don't believe me, call up a broker and ask what commission he'd charge on the purchase of four shares of IBM). Remember, too, that brokers charge an annual fee—typically $50—for acting as trustee beyond any fees for buying and selling stock.

Suggestion: Set up an IRA at a bank or mutual fund. When you accumulate at least $20,000—and you still have the itch to manage the investments yourself—switch the IRA to a broker.

Keogh Plans

A Keogh plan is like an IRA for full-time or part-time, self-employed persons. Anyone with income earned from their own profession or business may start a Keogh plan. The law, incidentally, does not consider interest and dividend income as self-employment income.

Banks, savings and loan associations, brokers, mutual funds, and insurance companies may all serve as custodians for Keogh plans. Most of the advantages (and disadvantages) of using them as custodians for IRAs apply to Keoghs as well. A Keogh plan may invest in pretty much anything, with the notable exception of "collectibles" such as coins, art, and memorabilia. **Even if you have an IRA and/or a private pension to shelter salaried income, nothing prevents you from setting up a Keogh to shelter self-employment income.**

Contributions to a Keogh are deductible from current income; interest accumulates tax-free within the account. There's a nasty tax penalty for withdrawals before age 59½ (unless you are totally disabled), or for failing to make adequate withdrawals after age 70½.

There are differences in Keoghs and IRAs as well as similarities. With a Keogh you may contribute up to 20 percent of your taxable income each year, up to a limit of $30,000.* That's a lot better than an IRA if you have substantial income. But the 20 percent ceiling cuts hard if you want to use a Keogh to shelter income from part-time self-employment.

Actually, there is a way around the 20 percent limit. Set up what's called a "defined benefit" plan rather than a regular "defined contribution" plan. The gimmick with a defined benefit plan is to tailor a savings schedule that, in theory, will permit you to collect a fixed monthly sum once you retire, much the way a private pension plan guarantees a fixed monthly payment. There are still limits on how much you can con-

*Thanks to the foggy bureaucratic language of the tax laws, there's been confusion about the percentage limit. Take my word: it really is 20 percent.

tribute to a defined benefit Keogh. They are based on actuarial formulas too complicated to explain here. If you have a large self-employment income and are eager to get the absolute maximum amount of tax shelter from a Keogh, consult a bank to see if a defined benefit plan is right for you. Remember, however, that the complexity makes defined benefit plans more expensive to set up and more expensive to maintain.

Along with the advantages of Keoghs comes one potential disadvantage. **If you have employees who have worked for you at least three years, you must include them in the plan on an equal percentage basis.** If you contribute 20 percent of your income to a Keogh, you must contribute 20 percent of theirs, too. That could work out well if you were planning to provide a generous tax-sheltered pension plan for your employees anyway. But it does limit the options.

Salary Reduction Plan

This is the last, but hardly the least, way to save for retirement later and enjoy tax breaks now. Since 1978 it has been possible for companies to deduct up to 10 percent of an employee's salary (at the employee's request) and put it in a trust, where it accumulates interest tax-free until retirement.

The tax reform law reduces the maximum annual contribution from $30,000 to $7,000, but that will only affect high-income earners willing and able to set aside a lot of cash. The reform law also tightens conditions on premature withdrawals. From now on, 401(k) plans will be treated pretty much like IRAs. Any withdrawal before age 59 will trigger ordinary income tax liability, plus a 10 percent tax penality. Withdrawals must begin by age 70, or Uncle Sam will levy a separate tax.

The only potential disadvantage to a salary reduction plan, beyond the inaccessibility of the money before retirement, is the possibility that it will reduce your Social Security benefits. Money stashed in an SRP is not counted as income. Thus unless you are earning more than the maximum income taxable for Social Security, an SRP will reduce your Social Security tax and, ultimately, your Social Security benefits.

Higher-income workers should hardly consider this a disadvantage. In hard dollars and cents, the gain from lower Social Security taxes would more than make up for the reduction in benefits. However, if you earn less than $12,000, the probable "return" on extra Social Security taxes paid is quite high. Since lower-income workers usually don't need a tax shelter anyway, the disadvantage of lower Social Security benefits may be decisive.

Not every company, alas, has a salary reduction plan. For many years that was because the regulations governing SRPs were so vague. Companies did not want to find out the hard way that they had run afoul of the IRS. Now, however, the rules have been clarified. If your company doesn't have a salary reduction plan, it's worth the trouble to find out why.

TIPS

$ The combination of lower tax rates on unsheltered income, plus new restrictions on deductibility, has made IRAs less attractive than they were before tax reform. However, most middle-income families will still find them a valuable means of saving for retirement.

$ Those who put safety and simplicity first will probably do best by putting their IRA money in a bank or savings and loan. Those willing to take bigger risks for a chance at a bigger gain should consider investing in a "family" of mutual funds.

$ High fees make both brokers and insurance companies poor choices for small IRAs.

$ Keogh plans provide self-employed professionals and operators of small businesses with even greater tax benefits than do IRAs.

$ If your company offers a salary reduction plan, and you can afford to save more for retirement, jump at the opportunity.

Bonus

SHOPPING THE FINANCIAL SUPERMARKETS

ONCE UPON A TIME stock brokers sold stocks and bonds, banks cashed checks and financed large purchases, real estate brokers hustled houses, insurance agents sold annuities, and credit card companies made small loans. Now it is all mixed up.

Nobody quite knows where the financial services industry is heading. Much depends on Congress, which is being pushed and pulled by dozens of competing interests. The rest depends on corporate America, which is rushing to stake out the new turf. One thing is sure, however. It is going to be very hard to halt the rise of the "financial supermarket," the combination broker/banker/insurance outlet.

One of these new consolidated service centers is, literally, in supermarkets. The Kroger chain started a dozen financial service centers inside its giant grocery stores. **Most, though, are metaphoric supermarkets— consolidated accounts combining credit card, checking, and brokerage services linked to the customer by a toll-free telephone number.** Is one right for you?

Consider first some generalities. The financial life of the average American is needlessly complicated. Decisions about insurance, checking, credit, savings, and house-buying are inevitably linked, but the person who advises you about one knows little about the others. At best the financial supermarkets should be able to offer consistent computer-based financial planning. At the very least they should be able to cut the confusion and inconvenience of record-keeping.

For the moment, however, the financial supermarkets have serious shortcomings. **None of them provides all the services you might need. And many provide an insufficient range of choices within the services they**

do offer. For example, Sears sells life insurance only from Allstate. Thus if you are making major financial decisions, you would still be wise to shop around.

What to look for:

Checking. Most integrated accounts let you write as many checks in sums as small as you want. But many provide only a monthly list of sums paid out, rather than cancelled checks. And some of these charge a service fee should you need a photocopy of a cancelled check as proof of payment.

Access to cash. Many banks allow round-the-clock access to your money through automated teller machines. Now some of the brokerage and investment houses with integrated accounts give you worldwide access to the machines by means of the VISA card or MasterCard networks. A super convenience.

Credit vs. debit cards. When is the credit card provided with the account not really a credit card? When it's a debit card. Using a debit card is like writing a check. The money is subtracted from your account the day the bill arrives. That's not so terrible; you'd have to pay the bill eventually (or pay interest on the balance) anyway. But it is nice to have the month of breathing room that true credit cards offer.

Fees. Somebody has to pay for all that service provided by integrated accounts. Surprise! That somebody is you. Make sure the account is worth the annual fee before signing up.

Minimum starting balances. Some integrated accounts allow you to start with $10,000. Others require $20,000 or more in cash and securities.

Interest. All integrated accounts pay interest on your cash. But some give you the option of keeping the money in a tax-exempt money market fund. Banks can provide government-insured money market accounts. Equally important is the issue of the "sweep." Some integrated accounts automatically transfer deposits into an interest-bearing account on the day they arrive. Others wait until the end of the week before sweeping the cash into a fund.

Broker services. Banks and discount brokers typically provide cheap discount brokering. But they probably won't provide advice on what to buy, and they may not be able to get you more sophisticated products, like zero-coupon bonds on tax-exempt unit trusts.

Frills. Everybody's got checking, brokering, interest, and charge cards. Some add nice things like free traveler's checks, home computer access, or statements cleverly designed to make life easier at tax time.

Here is a preliminary scorecard. In view of how fast the services are evolving, check carefully before putting your cash down.

Citibank. This aggressive giant has long chafed at the limits placed on the services it can sell. Hence it is not surprising that Citibank is one of the first banks to get serious about integrated financial accounts. A Citibank "Focus" account combines a checking account, an insured bank money market account, two different money market funds (run by The Landmark Group), a discount brokerage account (with Newbridge Securities), a VISA card, access to several hundred automated tellers in New York State, and a line of credit.

Note that the VISA card is a "debit" card. When you use it the money is automatically deducted from the cash balance in your account. Any use beyond that immediately sets the credit meter ticking. There are no insurance or annuity services sold. But Citibank will buy and sell precious metals, as well as T-bills, municipal bonds, stocks, and the like. A minimum of $10,000 in cash and securities is needed to open an account. The annual charge is $60.

Outside New York call (800) 752–0800. In New York State, dial (212) 752–8060.

Fidelity. Fidelity is an investment company that runs $20 billion in mutual funds. Its USA (Ultra Service Account) links a checking account, two money market funds, and discount brokerage services for a monthly fee of $3. The minimum balance to start is $10,000. Credit (not debit) cards are optional. The regular VISA card costs $24 a year; a Gold MasterCard is $36.

USA customers don't get advice on stocks. But they do get their cancelled checks back as well as a coded monthly statement which makes it easier to keep tax records. For those so inclined, Fidelity lets you buy and sell stock by home computer.

For information, call (800) 225–6190. In Massachusetts, call (617) 523–1919.

Merrill Lynch. Merrill Lynch, America's largest full-service broker, also has the most integrated financial accounts, here called Cash Management Accounts. For $75 a year you get a brokerage account, unlimited checking, taxable and tax-exempt money market funds, and a VISA debit card. Merrill Lynch's range of brokerage services are unusually broad by industry standards. If you can't buy it from Merrill Lynch, it hardly deserves to exist.

At $75 a year, a CMA is relatively cheap to maintain. But you must deposit $20,000 in cash or securities to begin, and *the VISA card provides no direct credit*. If you draw beyond the cash in your account, you must borrow against your securities and pay interest from day one. Merrill Lynch commissions are high, but you do get all the advice you want from your own account exec.

Phone (800) 221–4146. In New York State, try (800) 522–5510. In Hawaii, it's (800) 221–8802.

Prudential/Bache. This big financial conglomerate's Command Account offers the regular stuff, plus some clever gimmicks. There's a $10,000 minimum deposit in cash and/or securities to start. For a $50 annual fee you get unlimited checking linked to three money market funds, and a bank money market account (First Jersey National Bank). Or if you prefer, the stripped-down, Command Junior version ($30 a year) gives you 20 free checks annually. Pru-Bache's plastic is a VISA debit card from Banc One of Ohio. The card provides worldwide cash access through bank automated teller machines.

This is full-service brokering, so expect to pay high commissions in return for all the advice and access to fancy investment products. Special features include an annual recap statement listing all transactions, bill-paying by telephone for an extra fee, and free use of Compucard, a discount buying service for everything from appliances to prescription drugs to automobiles.

More information can be had from any local Prudential/Bache office. Or call (800) 222–4321.

Sears. Sears, America's biggest department store chain, owns Allstate Insurance, the Dean Witter full-service brokerage firm, the Coldwell Banker real estate brokerage firm, and Sears Savings and Loan. That means in California, where Sears S&L is chartered, Sears is able to provide banking, insurance, securities brokerage, and real estate sales under one roof. In one hundred or so stores with the Sears Financial Network outside California, there's no banking. But the combination of full-service brokerage, insurance, and real estate is nothing to sneeze at.

Sears' biggest drawbacks have already been mentioned: only Allstate insurance is for sale and all securities transactions are at full-service fees. **In other words, the price of convenience is limited selection.**

Shearson Lehman/American Express. The Financial Management Account offered by this full-service brokerage giant has an "upscale" tilt. The minimum initial deposit is $15,000 in securities and cash. The annual fee of $100 gets you unlimited checking, access to three money market funds, and an American Express Gold Card. The Gold Card is a true credit card with a line of credit. It provides access to a network of 1,500 automatic teller machines at banks, plus Amex traveler's check machines at airports.

The Financial Management Account isn't big in the gimmick department. But Shearson/Amex does send out a comprehensive annual statement, and allows you to code checks by 26 categories for record-keeping purposes.

Call local Shearson offices, or (800) 221–3636. In New York State, it's (800) 522–5429; in Hawaii and Alaska call (800) 221–1656.

Unified Management Corporation. This investment company's integrated account, called Unisave, offers a lot of service at a low price. The minimum initial deposit is just $1,000 in cash and securities. The money may be deposited in either a taxable or tax-free money market fund, with unlimited free checking for sums over $300. Smaller checks can be written, too—one free check a month for every $1,000 kept in the account. Beyond that number, you pay 30 cents a check. Cancelled checks are not automatically returned.

Funds can be switched into any of Unified Management's six no-load mutual funds, or used to buy securities at discount brokerage fees. Any fees paid—brokerage, extra check charges—offset the $60 annual cost of the account. So if you spent $40 on brokerage commissions, you would be billed only $20 more for the account.

Now for the interesting feature: You may transfer funds electronically from Unisave to your hometown bank account (or the other way round) for no additional charge.

As of this writing, Unisave does not include a credit card. But the management says a link with Visa is in the works. For information call (800) 862–7283.

PERSONAL ASSET INVENTORY

Checking and NOW Account	$ _____
Passbook Savings Account	_____
Bank Money Market Account	_____
Money Market Fund	_____
Credit Union Shares	_____
Other	_____

INSTANT ACCESS TOTAL $ _____

Treasury Bills	$ _____
U. S. Savings Bonds	_____
Bank Savings Certificates	_____
Stocks and Bonds	_____
Mutual Fund Shares	_____
GNMA Certificates	_____
Unit Trusts	_____

Life Insurance Cash Value _____

Other _____

LIQUID ACCESS TOTAL $ _____

IRA Account Balance $ _____

Keogh Account Balance _____

Salary Reduction Plan Balance _____

Annuity Account Balance _____

Vested Pension Rights _____

Est. Value of Autos
  (less loan balance) _____

Est. Value of House
  (less mortgage balance) _____

Est. Value of Other Real Estate
  (less mortgage balance) _____

Other _____

ILLIQUID ASSETS TOTAL $ _____

TOTAL ASSETS $ _____

Checking Account Overdrafts $ _____

Bank Loans Outstanding _____

Student Loans Outstanding _____

Credit Card Balance _____

Store Credit Balance _____

Est. Alimony or Child Support Liability _____

Taxes Due _____

Other Personal Liabilities _____

TOTAL LIABILITIES $ _____

ASSETS − LIABILITIES = NET WORTH $ _____

MORE BOOKS FOR YOUR MONEY

__STOCK MARKET PRIMER__
by Claude N. Rosenberg, Jr.   (K32-620, $4.95)

Lucidly written, Mr. Rosenberg shares with you the fundamental facts about investing: buying stocks and bonds, how the stock market works, spotting bull and bear markets, how to tell which industries have the greatest growth potential. Mr. Rosenberg takes the mystery out of the stock market and puts valuable, profit-making ideas at your disposal.

__HOW TO READ THE FINANCIAL PAGES__   (K30-066, $3.50, U.S.A.)
by Peter Passell   (K30-069, $4.50, Canada)

The world of securities has its own special language and the successful investor knows how to read it. This essential handbook explains every term and symbol found in the financial listings and fully describes the different kinds of securities that can be purchased.

__WHERE TO PUT YOUR MONEY 1986__   (K38-369, $3.95, U.S.A.)
by Peter Passell   (K38-370, $4.95, Canada)

Available in large-size quality paperback

Not long ago, the small investor had few choices—and he didn't make much money on his savings. He could open a passbook account at the bank, buy a government savings bond, or perhaps, get life insurance. Now the savings rules have changed, increasing both the opportunities and the risks. If you have time to read half a dozen newspapers and investment magazines every week you can sort out your optimum choices, but here's a simple, clear guide that will help you to zero in on what's best for you. Written by a former professor of economics at Columbia University, who is also a *New York Times* expert journalist and author of THE BEST, it is soundly based, comprehensive information.

__PERSONALIZED MONEY STRATEGIES__   (K30-115, $3.95, U.S.A.)
by Peter Passell   (K30-116, $4.95, Canada)

This guide is for those who believe that informed investors can do very well at the money game but understand that the chance for greater reward comes at the cost of greater risk. Passell's book lays out the principles, describes the investment tools, and suggests specific portfolios keyed to income, financial responsibilities and willingness to bear risk.

__PENNY STOCKS__
by Bruce G. Williams   (K38-010, $7.95)

Available in large-size quality paperback

Penny Stocks are pricednd that the chance for greater reward comes at the cost of greater risk. Passell's book lays out the principles, describes the investment tools, and suggests specific portfolios keyed to income, financial responsibilities and willingness future. PENNY STOCKS explains how it all works—and how you can be penny wise and pound rich!

WARNER BOOKS
P.O. Box 690
New York, N.Y. 10019

Please send me the books I have checked. I enclose a check or money order (not cash), plus 50¢ per order and 50¢ per copy to cover postage and handling.*
(Allow 4 weeks for delivery.)

_____ Please send me your free mail order catalog. (If ordering only the catalog, include a large self-addressed, stamped envelope.)

Name _____

Address _____

City _____

State _____ Zip _____

*N.Y. State and California residents add applicable sales tax.   96

LET WARNER BOOKS HELP YOU INVEST YOUR MONEY!

___**BOLD MONEY: A New Way**   *(K51-340, $16.95, U.S.A.)*
to Play the Options Game   *(K51-340, $24.75, Canada)*
by Melvin Van Peebles   Available in hardcover

This street-smart guide is devoted to the options game and how to make it work for you. It is a primer that gives you the knowledge you need to wisely and profitably enter the options arena, the exciting and potentially most lucrative area of the stock market.

___**MARTIN ZWEIG'S WINNING ON**   *(K51-234, $20.00, U.S.A.)*
WALL STREET   *(K51-234, $29.25, Canada)*
by Martin E. Zweig   Available in hardcover

The respected forecaster from *Wall Street Week* now shares his techniques for charting the market. He presents a simple, reliable and workable system for playing and beating the stock market. His methods are suitable for both conservative investors and more active traders. Extensively tested, his techniques are all verifiable and thoroughly documented in his book.

___**REAL WEALTH**
The Proven Strategy for a   *(K37-037, $9.95, U.S.A.)*
Lifetime of Guaranteed Income   *(K37-038, $13.50, Canada)*
by Wade Cook   Available in large-size quality paperback

The country's leading real estate entrepreneur unlocks the secrets to successful investing and turning real estate into a guaranteed income for life. It's certain to become one of the most exciting investment books of the 1980s.

___**THE OMEGA STRATEGY**   *(K32-634, $3.95, U.S.A.)*
by William David Montapert   *(K32-635, $4.95, Canada)*

The stock and commodity traders, money managers, and other professionals who have read this book say it is possibly the most sophisticated and definitely the most useful money book ever written. Author Montapert, a practicing attorney specializing in real estate investments, tax planning and money management, brings a new dimension of practicality to economic theory.

WARNER BOOKS
P.O. Box 690
New York, N.Y. 10019

Please send me the books I have checked. I enclose a check or money order (not cash), plus 50¢ per order and 50¢ per copy to cover postage and handling.* (Allow 4 weeks for delivery.)

_____ Please send me your free mail order catalog. (If ordering only the catalog, include a large self-addressed, stamped envelope.)

Name _____

Address _____

City _____

State _____ Zip _____

*N.Y. State and California residents add applicable sales tax.   178

Help Yourself and Your Career

___HOW TO MAKE A HABIT OF SUCCESS
by Bernard Haldane   *(K30-501, $3.50)*

The Haldane system is one of the most important success and self-improvement books recently published. Its self-identification process and Success Factor Analysis techniques have become integral to career planning programs in leading institutions such as Harvard and Columbia Universities and The Peace Corps. Change your career by using your personal interests and talents in a new way.

___POSITIONING: THE BATTLE FOR YOUR MIND
by Al Ries and Jack Trout   *(K32-897, $4.50, U.S.A.)*
                                    (K32-899, $5.95, Canada)

"Positioning" is the first body of thought to come to grips with the problems of communicating in an overcommunicated (too many companies, too many products, too many media, too much marketing noise) society.

You will learn in detail some unique concepts that can help you master the media: climbing the product ladder; *cherchez le creneau* (look for the hole); repositioning the competition; avoiding the no-name trap; and avoiding the line-extension trap.

___GETTING ORGANIZED   *large format paperback*
by Stephanie Winston   *(J38-344, $8.95, U.S.A.)*
                                   (J38-345, $11.95, Canada)

Guidelines to organization covering everything from financial to meal planning, maximization of storage space, living space and reduction of time required to complete everyday tasks.

___DRESS FOR SUCCESS   *large format paperback*
by John T. Molloy   *(K38-263, $7.95, U.S.A.)*
                                  (K38-264, $8.95, Canada)

The number-one book to make you look like a million so you can *make* a million will: make it easier for many men to sell everything better: open doors to the executive suite to men for whom they are now closed; make the right wardrobe less expensive; give women a simple, sensible guide to buying men's clothing; and teach men how women like them to dress.

WARNER BOOKS
P.O. Box 690
New York, N.Y. 10019

Please send me the books I have checked. I enclose a check or money order (not cash), plus 50¢ per order and 50¢ per copy to cover postage and handling.* (Allow 4 weeks for delivery.)

_____ Please send me your free mail order catalog. (If ordering only the catalog, include a large self-addressed, stamped envelope.)

Name _____

Address _____

City _____

State _____ Zip _____

*N.Y. State and California residents add applicable sales tax.   72

The Best of the Business from Warner Books

___IN SEARCH OF EXCELLENCE
Thomas J. Peters and   *(K38-389, $10.95, U.S.A.)*
Robert H. Waterman, Jr.   *(K38-390, $14.95, Canada)*
Highly acclaimed and highly optimistic about the future of American management, this essential book proves that American business is alive and
well—and successful! Subtitled "Lessons from America's Best-Run Companies," it reveals the secrets of the art of successful American management, the eight fascinating basic principles that the authors found hard at
work at Johnson & Johnson, Procter & Gamble, IBM, Hewlett-Packard,
Delta Airlines, McDonald's, and other well-run firms. Here are the native
American policies and attitudes that lead to growth and profits—policies and
attitudes that thousands of business people all over the country are now
trying for themselves!

___MEGATRENDS
Ten New Directions Transforming Our Lives
John Naisbitt   *(I32-922, $4.95, U.S.A.)*
                                                       (I32-923, $6.50, Canada)
Once in a great while a book so accurately captures the essence of its time
that it becomes the spokesman for that decade. In 1956 it was *The Organization Man*. In 1970 it was *Future Shock*. In the 1980's it will be *Megatrends*, the only "future" book whose predictions for tomorrow are based on
a dynamic analysis of what America is today. As Naisbitt details America's
shift from industrial production to providing services and information, you
can project your career and business moves. As you learn where the new
centers of activity are developing, you can decide where you should live. If
you have political goals, John Naisbitt's analysis of governmental trends
can help you target your energies. This is the challenge, the means, and the
method to better our lives . . . a must for everyone who cares about the
future.

WARNER BOOKS
P.O. Box 690
New York, N.Y. 10019

Please send me the books I have checked. I enclose a check or money order
(not cash), plus 50¢ per order and 50¢ per copy to cover postage and handling.*
(Allow 4 weeks for delivery.)

_____ Please send me your free mail order catalog. (If ordering only the
                catalog, include a large self-addressed, stamped envelope.)

Name _____

Address _____

City _____

State _____ Zip _____

*N.Y. State and California residents add applicable sales tax.   46

THE BEST FROM WARNER BOOKS

____**RE-INVENTING THE CORPORATION** *(K51-284, $17.50, U.S.A.)*
Transforming Your Job and *(K51-284, $24.50, Canada)*
Your Company for the New Information Society
by John Naisbitt and Patricia Aburdene

John Naisbitt (author of best-selling MEGATRENDS) and Patricia Aburdene reveal in their book how the corporation workplace is changing and how everyone can prepare for it. They have written a survival manual for established companies and a blueprint for entrepreneurs seeking to build the corporation of the future. They offer a guide to beginners who are looking for growth and success in an atmosphere of learning and fun. RE-INVENTING THE CORPORATION gives employees and employers alike the tools to help "re-invent" and get the most from career and company.

Available in Hardcover

____**A WHACK ON THE SIDE** *(K38-275, $9.95, U.S.A.)*
OF THE HEAD *(K38-276, $10.95, Canada)*
by Roger von Oech, Ph.D.

This important book zeros in on the ten mental locks that prevent you from being as innovative as you can be and shows you what you can do to open them. Combining wisdom, tomfoolery, paradox, philosophy, and scientific fact through stories, mental exercises, and case histories, the author distills his experiences as a creative thinking consultant for Apple, ARCO, DuPont, Xerox, etc. to help you discover why "a whack on the side of the head" can sometimes be the best thing for you.

WARNER BOOKS
P.O. Box 690
New York, N.Y. 10019

Please send me the books I have checked. I enclose a check or money order (not cash), plus 50¢ per order and 50¢ per copy to cover postage and handling.* (Allow 4 weeks for delivery.)

_____ Please send me your free mail order catalog. (If ordering only the catalog, include a large self-addressed, stamped envelope.)

Name _____

Address _____

City _____

State _____ Zip _____

*N.Y. State and California residents add applicable sales tax.   165

IMPROVE YOUR MANAGEMENT SKILLS WITH WARNER BOOKS!

____**WHAT THEY REALLY TEACH YOU AT**   (K38-317, $9.95, U.S.A.)
THE HARVARD BUSINESS SCHOOL   (K38-318, $13.50, Canada)
by Francis J. Kelly and Heather Mayfield Kelly
                                Available in large-size quality paperback.

What is a Harvard Business School education? Two HBS graduates offer all business people the concepts and methods that make this institution's graduates the most sought-after managers in the country. It offers what no other business book has ever offered before, and what every business person can use.

____**UP THE LADDER**   (K51-291, $17.95, U.S.A.)
Coping with the Corporate Climb   (K51-291, $26.25, Canada)
by Thomas Friedman   Available in hardcover.

Here are the stories of managers who cannot get by on gamesmanship, dress-for-success, or positive thinking alone. Friedman offers a brilliantly original and compassionate guide to real life on the corporate climb. Here is the opportunity to learn from the experiences of those who have climbed before you. It could be the most practical management book you will ever read.

____**THE ORGANIZED EXECUTIVE**
New Ways to Manage Time,   (K38-384, $8.95, U.S.A.)
Paper, and People   (K38-383, $11.95, Canada)
by Stephanie Winston   Available in large-size quality paperback.

This book is a basic tool for men and women in all professional spheres who want to get full value from their careers today. Learn how to design the office system and daily routine that's best for you, organize your files for ease and efficiency, combat procrastination with a solution that really works, and plan your business travel with practical tips.

____**THE 10-MINUTE ENTREPRENEUR**   (K38-069, $7.95, U.S.A.)
by Mark Stevens   (K38-070, $9.50, Canada)
                                Available in large-size quality paperback.

Ten minutes a day is all it takes to keep you and your company one step ahead of the game and on the fast track to more profits and more success. This book brings to you the sources of management insight and information for making and saving money on business ventures. By following the procedures outlined, you benefit from a team of the leading business consultants and authorities whose ideas and strategies are presented in this book.

WARNER BOOKS
P.O. Box 690
New York, N.Y. 10019

Please send me the books I have checked. I enclose a check or money order (not cash), plus 50¢ per order and 50¢ per copy to cover postage and handling.* (Allow 4 weeks for delivery.)

_____ Please send me your free mail order catalog. (If ordering only the catalog, include a large self-addressed, stamped envelope.)

Name _____

Address _____

City _____

State _____ Zip _____

*N.Y. State and California residents add applicable sales tax.   181

There's an epidemic with 27 million victims. And no visible symptoms.

It's an epidemic of people who can't read.

Believe it or not, 27 million Americans are functionally illiterate, about one adult in five.

The solution to this problem is you...when you join the fight against illiteracy. So call the Coalition for Literacy at toll-free **1-800-228-8813** and volunteer.

Volunteer Against Illiteracy. The only degree you need is a degree of caring.

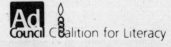

Ad Council   Coalition for Literacy

Warner Books is proud to be an active supporter of the Coalition for Literacy.